The Art of Drama, vol. 4

Jerusalem

PERIPETEIA PRESS

Published by Peripeteia Press Ltd.

First published November 2019

ISBN: **9781703364385**

All rights reserved. No part of this publication may be reproduced, stored in a retrieval system or in any form or by any means, without the prior permission in writing of the publisher, nor otherwise circulated in any form or cover other than that which it is published and without a similar condition including this condition being imposed on the subsequent publisher.

Check out our A-level English Literature website, peripeteia.webs.com

'Friends! Outcasts. Leeches. Undesirables. A blessing on you, and upon this beggar's banquet.'

Contents

Introduction	6
STAGECRAFT	13
DIALOGUE & CONVERSATIONAL ANALYSIS	44
THE NATURE OF THE PLAY	47
SETTINGS	
Location	52
The woods	53
Greece & the pastoral	54
Myth & fairy tale	57
Time era & Time when	60
CHARACTERS	
Johnny	64
Ginger	71
Phaedra	73
Tanya & Pea	75
Dawn & Marky	76
Davey & Lee	79

Fawcett & Parsons	81
The Professor	82
Troy	84
Wesley & the villagers	85
ACTION	88
STYLE	91
IDEAS	104
APPENDIX	108
GLOSSARY	133
ABOUT THE AUTHORS	137

Introduction to *The Art of Drama* series

The philosopher Nietzsche described his work as 'the greatest gift that [mankind] has ever been given'. The Elizabethan poet Edmund Spenser hoped his book *The Faerie Queene* would magically transform readers into noblemen. In comparison, our aims for The Art of Drama series of books are a little more modest. Fundamentally we aim to provide books that will be of maximum use to students of English and to their teachers.

In this new series of books, we aim to reproduce the success of our *The Art of Poetry* series by providing fine-grained, well-informed and engaging material on the key issues in key drama set texts. In the first book in the series, we focused on J. B. Priestley's popular old stager, *An Inspector Calls*. In the second, we turned our critical attention to Shakespeare's notoriously dark and troubling Scottish play, *Macbeth*. Our third book in the series will focus on *Hamlet* and in this edition we turn our attention to Jez Butterworth's riotous comedy, *Jerusalem*.

With the seemingly ever-increasing demands and importance of terminal exams, there's a great pressure on students and their teachers to reach top grades. One way to attempt to do this is to drill students with exam technique and fill their heads with information in the hope that they will be able to regurgitate it accurately in examinations. To us, that sort of approach eliminates an essential part of the experience of reading and writing about literature, perhaps the most rewarding and richest part of the experience, i.e. forming our own critical views. Good critical writing about poems, novels and plays at A-level does not merely repeat somebody else's ideas, rather it expresses the critical opinions of the writer, informed, of course, by their experiences in the classroom. No two essays on any Literary text should say exactly the same things. Ideally teaching should nurture pupils' ability to express their own critical thinking about texts in their own emerging critical voices, informed as we say by discussion with peers and the expertise of teachers.

Our GCSE books aim to inspire and enrich the literary experiences of pupils aimed for level 7 or thereabouts and above. This new *Jerusalem* guide is, however, aimed primarily at A-level students and their teachers. We hope and expect, though, that the material herein will prove to be interesting and useful to university students too.

Writing about plays

The play and the novel

Plays and novels have several significant features in common, such as characters, dialogue, plots and settings. In addition, pupils read plays in lessons, often sitting at desks in much the same way as they read novels. So it's not surprising that many pupils treat these two related, but distinct, literary art forms as if they were indistinguishable. Time and again, teachers and examiners come across sentences such as 'In the novel *Macbeth*…' Though sometimes this can be just a slip of the pen, often this error is a good indicator of a weak response. Stronger responses fully appreciate the fact that *Macbeth* is a play, written for the stage, by a playwright and realise the implications of the writer's choice of the dramatic form.

Characterisation

Imagine you're a novelist writing a scene introducing a major character. Sit back and gratefully survey the rich variety of means at your disposal: You could begin with a quick pen portrait of their appearance, or you could have your characters say or do something significant. Alternatively, you could use your narrator to provide comments about, and background on, the character. Then again, you might take us into the character's thoughts and reveal what's really going on inside their head. If you're trying to convey thought as it happens, you could follow the Modernists and employ a stream of consciousness.

Now imagine that you're a playwright. Sit up and survey the far more limited means at your disposal. Though you could describe a character's appearance, you'd have to communicate this through stage directions, which, of course, a theatre audience would not be able to read or hear. The same holds true for background information and narratorial style comments about the character. And unless you're going to use the dramatic devices known as the aside and the soliloquy, as famously Shakespeare did in his great tragedies, you'll struggle to find a direct way to show what your character's really thinking. As a playwright, action and dialogue, however, are your meat and drink. For a novelist being able to write dialogue is a useful skill; for a dramatist it's essential, the sine qua non.

In general, drama focuses our attention on the outward behaviour of characters. Skillfully done, this can, of course, also reveal interior thoughts. Nevertheless, novels more easily grant us access to the workings of the mind. You may have noticed this when novels are adapted into films and directors have to make the decision about whether to use a voiceover to convey the narrator or characters' thoughts. Rarely does this work uncheesily well.

Settings

With a swish of his or her pen or deft fingers over a keyboard, a novelist can move quickly and painlessly from one setting to another. One chapter of a novel could be set in medieval York, the next leap to a distant planet in the distant future. The only limitation is the novelist's skill in rendering these worlds. What is true for geographical settings is also true for temporal ones. A novelist can write 'One hundred years later…' or track a character from cradle to grave, or play around with narrative time, using flashbacks and flashforwards.

Though a little more restricted, a modern film director can also move fairly easily between geographical and temporal settings and can cross-cut between them. Not so a playwright. Why? Because plays are written for an actual physical stage and radically changing a stage set during the action of a play is a tricky and potentially cumbersome business. Imagine you've written a play set in the middle ages. Your stageset is a medieval village green - ramshackle thatched huts, pig pens and dirty streets and authentic medieval smells. But you next scene takes place somewhere very different. How are you going to transform the medieval green to the dizzyingly futuristic world of the Planet Zog in 2088 A.D.?

Possibly you could get your stage technicians to dismantle and construct the different stage sets while the audience waits patiently for the action to restart. But wouldn't that be clumsy, and rather break the spell you'd hope your play was weaving? More likely you'd use a break, perhaps between scenes or, better, during the interval for any major re-arrangement of stage scenery.

Practically speaking, how many different stage sets could you create for a single play? Minimalistic stage designs might allow you to employ more settings, but you'd still be far more restricted than a film director or a novelist. And then there's the cost. Theatres aren't usually loaded with money and elaborate stage sets are likely to be expensive. Another way out of this would be to have a pretty much bare and unchanging stage set and convey changes in scenes through the dialogue, a technique Shakespeare often employs:

Character 1: What is this strange, futuristic place?
Character 2: Why, this must be the capital city of the Planet Zog.

Etc.

[Only Shakespeare is a little more subtle than that, naturally.]

Plays also tend to be written chronologically, i.e. with time always moving forward. Partly this is because as we watch plays in real time, it's difficult to convey to an audience that a particular scene is actually a flashback and is set in the past. There are exceptions, of course, to the chronological trend. Notably Harold Pinter's *Betrayal*, for instance, in which the action of the play unfolds backwards from the present to past.

The time frame of a play also tends to be limited – days, weeks, perhaps even months, but very rarely years, decades or centuries. After all, it's not easy for an actor, or series of actors, to convincingly present characters aging over a prolonged period.

The stage and the page

Physicists and chemists have many things in common, as do rugby and football players and vets and doctors. Novelists and playwrights also have many things in common, but they work in distinctly different fields. You wouldn't want a chemist teaching you physics, ideally, or depend on a rugby player to score a crucial FA cup goal. Nor would you want a vet to operate on you if you were ill, or for your GP to treat your darling pet. And, with only a few exceptions, nor would you want to read a novel written by a playwright or witness a play written by a novelist. Precious few writers excel in both literary forms [Samuel Beckett, Chekhov and Michael Frayn come to mind, but few others] which underlines the point about the different demands of writing for the stage and for the page.

Novels take place in the theatre of the reader's mind; plays take place in an actual physical space, on an actual physical stage and in real time. For the latter to happen a whole load of other people other than the writer have to be involved – directors, actors, designers, producers, technicians and so forth. And this takes us right to the heart of another crucial difference between reading a play, reading a novel and seeing a play on a stage.

When we're reading a novel, the novelist can fill in the details of what is happening around the dialogue, such as gestures made by the characters:

'Did they even have pig-pens in medieval York?' asked Mikey, cocking his left eyebrow in a typically quizzical manner.

When we **read** a play, sometimes these details are apparent from stage directions. However, we cannot see what characters are doing while other characters are speaking and we can easily forget that silent characters are present in a scene. When we **watch** a play, however, actors reveal how their characters are reacting to what others are saying, and often these reactions convey crucial information about relationships, feelings and atmosphere.

Without this visual dimension it is all too easily for readers to ignore the things that are supposed to be happening in the narrative background while each character is speaking. If a play on a page is similar to a musical score, awaiting performance, a play on the stage is like the concert itself.

Focusing on the dramatic devices used by a playwright has a double benefit: Firstly, all good analytical literary essay concentrate on the writer's craft; secondly, such a focus emphasises to the examiner that you understand the nature of the type of text you're exploring - a play - and distinguishes you from many other readers who don't really appreciate this crucial fact. In the next section we'll sharpen our focus on the playwright's craft by honing in on stagecraft.

Stagecraft

When writing about a novel it's always productive to focus on narration. Narration includes narrative perspective, such as first and third person, types of narrator, such as naïve and unreliable, as well as narrative techniques, such as the use of dialogue, cross-cuts and flashbacks. Narration is worth focusing your attention on because it's an absolutely integral feature of all novels and short stories. In plays the equivalent of narration is stagecraft. Examining stagecraft is an incisive and revealing way to focus on the writer at work. Some playwrights are able to use all the craft and resources of the theatre, namely set, props, costumes, lighting and music, while for various reasons [technical, artistic, budgetary] other playwrights may be more restricted.

Shakespeare, for instance, doesn't really use lighting in his plays, except notably in *The Winter's Tale*, because most of his plays were performed at the Globe theatre in daylight. His instructions on costume are also very limited, usually embedded within the texts, rather than stated separately in stage directions. Think, for example, of Malvolio's yellow cross-gartered stockings or Hamlet's inky suit of woe. On the other hand, the importance of costumes is underlined repeatedly in Shakespeare's plays by characters who disguise themselves by changing their clothes. For instance, Viola becoming Cesario in *Twelfth Night* or Kent and Edmund disguising themselves in *King Lear*. Repeatedly too, villainy in Shakespeare's plays tries to remain hidden under a layer of fine clothes.

When a playwright is restricted in the range of stagecraft he or she can utilise, not only do the devices they employ become more prominent, but other integral aspects of stage business also become more significant. In *Macbeth*, as in *An Inspector Calls*, for instance, exits and entrances are particularly important. Indeed the managing of exits and entrances is at the core of all plays. Exits facilitate changes in costume and allow actors to recover from, or prepare for, major scenes. Tracking these seemingly simple instructions always uncovers interesting and significant patterns, particularly in terms of which characters know what information at crucial points in the action. Think, for instance, how rarely Johnny Byron is off stage and what he misses when he is absent.

Stage sets

As we mentioned in our discussion of the key differences between novels and plays, the latter invariably have fewer settings due to the fact that dramatic texts have to be physically realised in stage designs. And, as we also noted, changing from one elaborate stage set to another presents problems for directors and, potentially for the finances of a production. What sort of choices does a stage designer have to make when creating a set? Firstly, a lot depends on the nature of the play, as well as the playwright, the director and the budget. Some playwrights are very particular about the settings of their plays and describe them in tremendous detail.

The American playwright Tennessee Williams, for instance, wrote particularly poetic stage directions, such as those that open his play *A Streetcar Named Desire*: 'First dark of an evening in May' and the 'sky is a peculiarly tender blue, almost turquoise, which invests the scene with a kind of lyricism and gracefully attenuates the atmosphere of decay'. If that isn't enough to get a stage designer shake and scratch their head, Williams finishes with a synesthetic poetic flourish 'you can almost feel the warm breath of the brown river' that is even more challenging to realise on stage.

Other playwrights will sketch out far more minimalistic sets. Samuel

Beckett in *Waiting for Godot*, for instance, describes the stage set in the sparest way possible, using just six simple words: 'A country road. A tree. Evening'. [Despite the skeletal detail, in production, Beckett was notoriously specific and exacting about how he wanted the stage to be arranged.]

Even if the playwright doesn't provide a great deal of information about the exact setting, a director is likely to have an overall concept for a play and insist, albeit to varying degrees, that the set design fit with this. If, for instance, a director wishes to bring out the contemporary political resonances of a play such as *Julius Caesar* she or he might dress the characters like well-known American politicians and set the play in a place looking a little like the modern White House. Similarly, Shakespeare's *Richard III* has often been relocated to an imagined modern fascistic state.

Given free reign, a stage designer has to decide how realistic, fantastical, symbolic and/or expressionist their stage set will be. The attempt to represent what looks like the real world on stage, as if the audience are looking in through an invisible fourth wall, is called verisimilitude and is the equivalent of photographic realism in fine art.

The stage sets for *Jerusalem*

In the prologue to Act One Butterworth provides a lot of information about the stage set. Initially we are presented with a traditional proscenium arch stage, revealed via a curtain on which is painted a *faded* Cross of St. George [our italics]. This proscenium arch is 'adorned' with images of 'cherubs', 'woodland scenes. Dragons. Maidens. Devils. Half-and-half creatures.' In addition, draped across the beam is a sign, reading 'THE ENGLISH STAGE COMPANY'.
What key ideas are established here?

Firstly, from the onset, the theme of England and Englishness is signaled by the curtain and banner, as, less obviously, is the importance to the play of the story of St. George and the Dragon [also indicated by the images of dragons and maidens on the proscenium]. The fact that the flag is 'faded' suggests perhaps tiredness, old age and lost vitality, ideas that will be reinforced by the props littered about in the first scene.

Secondly the conventional proscenium arch emphasises *Jerusalem's* rich theatricality while also connecting it to traditional plays of the English stage. On the other hand, the banner headline links the play explicitly to the modern and politically radical Royal Court theatre and its house company of that name. The impression of doubleness in these references to both the traditional and the radical stage is picked up in the contrasting details on the proscenium arch itself; cherubs and devils, dragons and maidens. Most tellingly, of course, are the 'half-and-half creatures', figures that foreshadow the play's characters and especially its shape-shifting, simultaneously super and sub-human protagonist, Johnny Byron. Indeed, for the people of the New Estate, the Kennet and Avon council, and for some readers and critics Byron is a kind of folk devil. In addition, through evoking the Saint George and the Dragon story, Butterworth will make us wonder whether Johnny is the saint or the dragon.

Once the curtain rises for a second time a new scene is presented to us. The very first word of Butterworth's stage directions is 'England'.

We then see a 'clearing in a moonlit wood' and the time is specifically 'midnight'. At the back of the clearing is an '*old* forty-foot mobile home' [these, and all subsequent italics are ours] with a front door and porch. Later we will see that this mobile home has a hatch at the top, as well as two large speakers attached to its roof. From one end flies the '*old* Wessex flag' of a golden dragon and an '*old rusted* railway sign', reading 'Waterloo', has been screwed to the front of the home.

In the mobile home's porch, littered about, is a lot of 'junk'. Almost all of these props are described as 'old': 'an old mouldy couch'; 'an old hand-cranked air-raid siren'; 'an old submarine klaxon'; 'an old record player'; 'an old American-style fridge'; 'an old windchime'. Like the railway sign, there's also a swing-ball set that is 'rusty'.

So what have we got here exactly? What is being signaled by the stage set? Obviously, Englishness and English identity is once again being emphasized, with hints at potential rebellion and appetite for battle through the Waterloo sign and the dragon flag, as well suggestions of more localized notions of identity in the reference to Wessex. Like the 'faded' curtain, there's a suggestion of an old, historical sense of Englishness. 'Oldness' can, of course, be double-edged, carrying both positive and negative meanings. Mostly these props appear to be signaling 'old' in the negative sense of tired out, worn down, decrepit, useless, carrying similar connotations to that other adjective Butterworth uses, 'rusty'. However, as we will discover, some of these old objects – the klaxon, the air-raid siren and the record player - still function, warning us, perhaps, that what might appear old, outdated and redundant in this play might turn out to be both valuable and potent.

Ostensibly a 'clearing in a moonlight wood' might imply a lovely, rather romantic setting. We know from literature that this is the sort of special place and the sort of special light in which strange and magical things might happen. Indeed, it sounds like a stage direction from one of Shakespeare's comedies. However this impression is countered by the 'deafening bass' pumping from the mobile home. If the opening lines of Butterworth's stage directions briefly suggest a tranquil, pastoral setting, the subsequent details - thumping music and wild dancing – smash that impression into pieces. Yet these, in turn give way to just 'birdsong', a clear symbol of pastoral peacefulness.

As with the devils and cherubs, the traditional and radical stage, the obsessively deployed double-edged adjective 'old', the thumping music and the birdsong, the stage set embodies ideas in conflict, a disorientating half-and-halfness. Yes, this is a pastoral setting. But woods in literature can also take on darker associations; think, for example, of fairy tale witches, wolves and ogres; is Johnny's mobile home a kind of modern witch's house? Moreover, has this potentially pastoral setting been polluted and despoiled by the presence of the old mobile home and all the accompanying decaying detritus littered around it? Certainly the officials from the Kennet and Avon council think so. But, conversely, this place could be seen as an alternative way of living, a home deeply rooted in nature, deeply rooted in Englishness, making use of junk most of us would casually throw away.

It's curious that in this context Butterworth includes a couple of pieces of Americana – the large fridge and the Coca-Cola plastic chairs. While the Watermill Theatre production in 2018 used a very battered 1970's English Sprite caravan, in contrast, picking up on the other American details, the original Royal Court production used a run-down American-style Airstream caravan for mobile home. Do these American details suggest a more complex, perhaps hybrid, sense of identity or imply that something has been tainted through the incursions of American consumerism even into the deep inner recesses of an English wood? As we will see as the play progresses, despite Johnny's best efforts to maintain his sanctuary, the exterior world will press and impinge on him and eventually leave an indelible mark.

Other stage directions

Most playwrights include stage directions within their scripts. By convention written in italics, these directions often establish the setting of a scene, outline lighting or music, convey physical action and sometimes also indicate to the actors how lines should be spoken. In *Who's Afraid of Virgina Woolf*, for example, the playwright, Edward Albee provides lots of extra information alongside the actual words his characters say. Here's a short extract to illustrate the point [in the extract a married woman, Martha, is flirting outrageously with a younger married man, Nick, in front of both his wife, Honey and Martha's own husband, George]:

MARTHA	[*to George…still staring at Nick, though*]: SHUT UP! [*Now, back to Nick*] Well, have you? Have you kept your body?
NICK	[*unselfconscious… almost encouraging her*]: It's still pretty good. I work out.
MARTHA	[*with a half-smile*]: Do you!
NICK	Yeah.
HONEY	Oh, yes…he has a very…firm body.
MARTHA	[*still with that smile… a private communication with Nick*] Have you! Oh, I think that's very nice.

Through the stage directions, Albee indicates to the actors where characters are looking, who they are at addressing at different points, the tone they should adopt and even the facial expression the actors should put on. In addition, he uses capital letters as well as punctuation to convey tone and VOLUME. By way of contrast, Shakespeare's stage directions are minimalistic. As we've noted, at the start of scenes Shakespeare establishes the setting with a just a few bold strokes of his quill and often, within scenes he embeds stage directions within dialogue.

Butterworth uses a variety of stage directions. Only occasionally do these comprise instructions as to how a line should be read. When Parsons fails to rouse Byron through his knocking in Act One, for instance, Fawcett responds by only saying her partner's name and Parsons replies to her with just one word, 'ma'am'. Without Butterworth's stage directions – 'rebuking' and 'apologetic' - it would be hard to pick the tone and implied power dynamics he wanted here. Later Butterworth specifies that Ginger should speak 'innocently' [although his comment about Johnny being barred from The Coopers Inn is actually mock innocent] and in that in Act Two Dawn should speak 'flatly' when telling Marky to say goodbye to his father. The general absence of these instructions indicate that Butterworth trusts his own script, the skill of actors and the intelligence of the audience. If all three are strong, then such instructions are unnecessary.

Take, for example, Marky's response to his mother's request to say farewell to a father he rarely sees and who, in this scene, has been trying to use his magnetic charisma on his son, without any success. Byron's son, Marky, says just one word, 'goodbye'. It's the most minimal, functional and merely perfunctory response imaginable. What Marky doesn't say speaks volumes; there is no affection, no reference to 'dad', or even 'father' or even 'Johnny'. And, if the actor or the audience hadn't picked up Marky's numb, flat, stand-offish tone, Butterworth adds an embedded stage action to underscore the point: Johnny: 'You gonna give me a hug before you go? No? Suit yourself'.

Sometimes seemingly simple and straightforward stage directions are used to say a lot. In the same scene from Act Two, for instance, Byron's wife, Dawn has been trying to distance herself from her former husband and his self-destructive, dissolute lifestyle. Dawn has got a proper job, has a new boyfriend, has joined mainstream society. She knows that she has had to grow-up. She has a child to look after and she has been upbraiding Johnny about his responsibilities, using the only leverage she has, her son. But, in such close physical proximity to Johnny Dawn's resolve begins to waver. She allows Johnny to search her bag, she 'does a couple of lines' and then 'walks away' to retain her sense of distance. But then, as Johnny asks her about her new boyfriend, the stage directions inform us that 'He moves to her. Smiles'. Butterworth doesn't need to tell us how Dawn responds; if she'd moved away, he would have told us so. Next Johnny 'touches her hair'. Her resistance is unconvincing and feeble, 'Get off me. It's too hot'. He is not deterred. 'He kisses her'. In all this stage action so far, Johnny has been the instigator and Dawn the passive recipient. No, not entirely passive as her not moving away from him is an action. Crucially, though the next stage direction shifts simply in pronouns to 'they kiss', before once again Dawn tries to separate herself 'she pulls away'. Such action, tender, sexually-charged, delicate, beautifully conveys Dawn's conflicted feelings and Johnny's continuing charm.

This intimate, two-handed scene culminates in perhaps the most brilliantly theatrical, startling and mysterious moment in the whole play. Like a hypnotist, Johnny makes Dawn look deep into his eyes. What does she see there? 'Black'. And then he tells to look 'deeper' because he is going to show her something. What she sees we'll never know, of course, but whatever it is, it has a profound effect on her. She is literally shaken and leaves the clearing still 'trembling'. Moments later, once Dawn has left, the stage directions tells us that Johnny is entirely on his own for the only time so far in the play and he smiles to himself. Then, tellingly, 'he stops smiling'. Then he 'eyes the wood nervously'. In this private moment we see behind the mask of Johnny's bravura and defiance to the more vulnerable and perhaps even frightened character within.

Butterworth's handling of comic stage action is often particularly entertaining. Frequently the action is most entertaining when something unexpected and previously hidden is suddenly revealed. In the opening scenes, for instance, a considerable amount of time has already elapsed before, woken by a blast of the horn, Lee suddenly sits up, having apparently been asleep on the couch. Similarly, a little later, Pea and Tanya wake and emerge groggily from under Byron's mobile home. Near the end of Act One, which might be approximately forty-five minutes of stage time, a conversation develops involving bartering a tortoise for drugs. The conversation culminates when Johnny, somewhat improbably, reaches into his jacket and pulls out the aforesaid tortoise, which it seems he has kept handily on his person for just this sort of occasion. Similarly, in Act Two when Johnny's far-fetched tale of having met the giant who built Stonehenge is met with understandable skepticism by Ginger, 'Where's this giant's drum? His earing. Where's that then?' Johnny reveals that Ginger has been 'sitting on it' and this drum/seat has, in fact, been on stage, unnoticed, during the whole of the play. There are hidden and perhaps magical depths to Rooster's home, it seems. And, from the start, we also know that somewhere hidden from our view is the young, missing girl, Phaedra Cox.

Indeed, at other times the stage action is far less comical. For example, when Phaedra's disappearance is first mentioned by the other girls, Johnny begins chopping wood with an axe. While the girls share genuine concern for Phaedra's wellbeing with Lee and Ginger, in the background Johnny is bringing an axe down hard and splitting logs:

LEE: Phaedra. Her mum said she ain't been home for days.
JOHNNY splits a log.

In fact, Johnny repeats this violent, ominous action four times during this brief dialogue. Having laughed at and been richly entertained by Johnny and his gaggle of ne'er-do-wells, the audience may start to wonder whether there might be something much darker and more disturbing going on, hitherto covered over by all the comic antics.

Of course, the tragic aspect of this tragicomedy really begins to dominate the play's action with the arrival of Troy. Once Troy is onstage the atmosphere immediately darkens and the air almost audibly crackles with tension. There is a palpable sense of threat, of potential violence only just held back, on the cusp of being released. For the first time in a play that often seems to whizz along in a voluble, free-wheeling, knockabout style, Butterworth uses frequent uncomfortable pauses, awkward silences and hyphens between dialogue:

GINGER: Sorry.
Pause.

Pause
TROY: What did you say?
Pause

Pause. The others look ashamed. Exit Troy. Silence.

The hyphens indicate Troy's coiled-spring impatience and are embedded stage directions, telling the actor playing Troy to aggressively interrupt Johnny. Other embedded stage directions underline Johnny's failed attempts to play host and placate him: 'Pull up a chair Lee'; 'Shift up girls. Make room'; 'Let's have a drink' – offers of hospitality Troy bluntly refuses. Butterworth doesn't have to write stage directions telling the actor playing Troy to remain standing, menacing, glowering at Johnny; it is implied by the dialogue.

The next time Butterworth brings Troy back onto the stage he comes, of course, with his henchmen. And they inflict a terrible beating on Johnny Obviously, this would be a very difficult scene to stage convincingly, and probably would be unbearable for any audience to witness live. In some ways, leaving it to our imaginations actually makes it worse. Once we have clocked that the two men have a 'branding iron' and a 'blow torch' [props recalling a dragon's fire] our minds jump immediately to the worst. Butterworth's stage directions, 'we can hear and sense an awful beating taking place' and a 'single bellow of pure pain', 'and again' are horribly visceral and the stage direction 'eventually' makes us wait to see the worst, increasing our sense of dread. Then the men open the door and run away. We hear sounds from the fair. The atmosphere is a little unreal, 'dreamlike', with, for us, horribly incongruous laughter drifting over from the fair 'on the wind'. Eventually Johnny staggers out, broken-bodied, bleeding with 'on both cheeks, charred and bloody 'X's'. Read on a page this description is potent enough; seen live, on stage, this image of a battered and scarred Johnny will not be easily forgotten.

Props

Props can, of course, be used in all manner of ways. In Arthur Miller's *The Crucible* at the climax of the play the protagonist, John Proctor signs a false confession of having committed witchcraft on a piece of paper. But when he is asked to give up this parchment by the court officials he will not, and his final defiance is shown dramatically when he tears this prop in half. In Shakespeare's tragedy *King Lear*, the physical ring of the crown is an emblem of the impossibility of splitting the kingdom successfully between Lear's daughters and therefore of the foolishness of the king's plan. In many of Shakespeare's plays props in the form of physical letters are intercepted and fall dangerously into the wrong hands, moving on the plot.

Props can also be used as signals of character - heroes in Shakespeare's plays invariably brandish swords, while fops carry nosegays. Most of the villains carry bottles of poison. Props can be used to heighten a dramatic effect and, as in the example from *The Crucible* to tell in a single image or action something it would take words longer to do.

Before you read the next section list any props you can remember appearing in *Jerusalem*. Try to arrange them in chronological order. Then write next to each one how they are used by the dramatist. Here are the most important props from Act One:

- Old air-raid siren
- Old submarine klaxon
- Old record player
- Stacks of old LPs
- Loudhailer

The Russian playwright and short story writer Anton Chekhov wrote that if a play features a gun as a prop in its first scene then at some point later in the play the gun needed to be fired. By this Chekhov meant that the seemingly incidental details of a story or play must have a function; otherwise they are merely decorative and therefore redundant. The various forms of sirens, horns and klaxons go off regularly during the action of the play, predominantly to comic effect. Johnny lets off the first deafening blast of the airhorn into a loudhailer in response to the 'attack' of the two council reps. A little later Ginger lets off the air-horn, seemingly at random, startling Lee awake. At the end of Act One, having decided against going to the Flintock Fair, Johnny 'winds the siren defiantly'. As Johnny's rag-tag troops gather at the start of Act Two, Lee 'sounds the submarine' klaxon before Johnny channels Shakespeare's *Henry the Fifth* rallying his army before Agincourt. Although comical, these regular blasts of sounds designed as warnings of imminent attack foreshadow the battles Byron will face, with the Kennet and Avon Council, with the police and with Troy. Ironically, when he most needs to be warned, the horn and klaxon do not go off. Both times Troy arrives in the clearing he is, at first, unnoticed by Johnny.

The old record player and the LPs will come into their own in the penultimate scene of the play as Phaedra and Johnny are finally seen together and dance closely while for both of them time is quickly running out. It's an intimate, disturbing scene, with the suggestion of sexual attraction between the two characters, the middle-aged man and teenage girl. And discovering them dancing seems to confirm Troy's fears and, for him, justify his violent retribution.

- Assorted empty bottles, cups, plates & pint glasses
- Bottle of vodka, bottle of whiskey, flask, spliffs

These props are used consistently, throughout the play, to indicate that the characters are continually 'giving it long-handle' in Davey's terms. Johnny Byron, in particular, downs bottles of spirits, smokes joints, does lines of cocaine. Looked at from one perspective, this might seem a life of wild, intoxicated, unabashed hedonism. From another perspective this behaviour is self-indulgent, irresponsible, purposeless and self-destructive. Certainly the 'puritans' of the New Estate and mainstream society share the latter view. However, when representatives from outside the wood enter Johnny's domain – notably Dawn and Wesley – they partake in the intoxication and illegal drug-taking, suggesting some hypocrisy on the puritan side of the argument.

Left scattered around the clearing, these props perhaps also signal the despoiling of a natural, potentially pastoral, environment. Or they suggest a communal, carefree abandon and a lack of interest in material belongings, depending on how you see it.

- Mars bar

Johnny is adept at using mundane details to give his outrageous stories some grounding in reality. Having told a preposterous story about a night of passion with the member of Girls Aloud to a skeptical Ginger, Johnny retrieves a Mars Bars and throws it to Ginger. Despite his skepticism, 'Ginger looks at it, then instinctively drops it as if it's unclean', a stage direction that conveys the extraordinary persuasive power of Johnny's storytelling. Even more impressively, Johnny will later pull off a similar trick with the giant's drum earing.

- Lighter
- Smashed TV set

Byron uses the lighter to light his joints and later to set fire to both the Kennet and Avon council notice of eviction and finally his own mobile home. It's a simple prop, but connects him with potential damage and destruction as well as, crucially, to fire. The latter association feeds into the unresolvable question in the play about whether Johnny or Troy is the dragon in the story of Saint George, the story that ripples beneath the surface as an ever-present subtext to *Jerusalem*. In the Royal Court production Mark Rylance also rather brilliantly used the lighter to represent his own human stature in comparison to that of a giant when Johnny is telling that tallest of tall stories.

The smashed TV set also reminds us of Johnny's potential destructive violence and the potentially damaging, despoiling consequences of the excesses of the forest parties. Significantly, Johnny cannot even remember the violence and the destruction he himself has wreaked. Arguably smashing the TV set also symbolically implies the violent rejection of conventional, mainstream and passive forms of entertainment. In this reading, in effect, the broken TV set becomes a metonym for a rejected and smashed up culture.

- Accordion

Music, of course, features prominently in the play; a rich mixture of music, as we'll discuss a bit later. The accordion seems an improbable and incongruous object in this woodland clearing, but connects Davey to older, more authentic forms of culture and entertainment.

- Mobile phone

Butterworth must be one of the first playwrights to realise the dramatic potential of the mobile phone. Phones and phone calls have long featured in plays – we might think of the crucial phone calls in *An Inspector Calls* for instance. But Butterworth's use of a mobile phone is novel. Its effect is to make us watch characters on stage watching something else, drawing out attention to watching and witnessing an improbable event. The fact that we can only hear the audio recording turns it into another form of storytelling, like a radio play, and we are encouraged to use our imaginations to fill in the visual detail. The stage direction, 'sound of a man smashing up his TV with a cricket bat' must have had the Royal Court's sound technicians scratching their heads.

Later in the play, Dawn has to use Johnny's mobile phone because the one he had bought her for a birthday present 'got cut off' because he has failed to keep up the payments. This seems emblematic of their relationship and of Johnny's unreliability as a husband and father. Pointedly Dawn deletes the number she rings to prevent Johnny from intruding further into the life she is trying to build.

- Camera
- Clipboard & case
- Digital video camera
- Staple gun
- Paper

All of the above props are carried about by Fawcett and Parsons, the officials from the local council. Alongside their high-viz jackets these objects signify the characters' official roles of writing, recording, documenting events and enforcing the council's will; they make manifest their seemingly legitimate powers. Crucially, of course, Parsons offer to delete a piece of inconvenient footage indicates the power imbalance being enacted in *Jerusalem* as well as the potential for the forces of law and order to behave corruptly and without accountability. Fawcett and Parsons will be the ones recording, documenting and presenting their version of these events once Johnny and all his great ephemeral eloquence has been wiped from the woods.

- Lee's ticket

Lee's ticket is emblematic of the need for the characters in the play to move on and the continual frustration of that need. A Peter Pan figure, Johnny needs to grow up and leave behind a protracted adolescence. As Dawn opines, Johnny is living in a dreamworld and needs to 'wake-up, because the 'world turns. And it turns. And it moves on and you don't. You're still here'. Described as a 'lost boy', Ginger has been stuck in the same routines for years. The Professor is caught in a melancholic loop, continually searching for something or someone he has lost, perhaps his dog, perhaps his wife, perhaps, as his inability to distinguish Ginger from a woman suggests, his own mind. Davey's life follows the same soul-destroying and life-limiting routines, so much so that he tries desperately to encourage his best friend to escape. And Phaedra, of course, may be literally trapped, possibly kidnapped and held captive by Johnny or possibly sheltering under his protection from an abusive stepfather.

- Axe

We have already discussed Butterworth's use of the axe, with Johnny chopping firewood when the conversation in the clearing turns to Phaedra. As with the lighter and the cricket bat, the axe reminds us of Johnny's potentially dangerous, violent side. Apparently in the Royal Court, presumably defying just the sort of Health and Safety legislation that real life Fawcett and Parsons might be tasked with enforcing, Mark Rylance used a real axe and not just a blunt stage dummy one. Hence the actor actually split logs with a real, sharp blade, adding an extra frisson of realism and danger to the play.

- A tortoise

Whether a real live tortoise or a dummy one was used in the play is unknown by the authors of this guide. However, the moment when this creature/ prop is revealed from Johnny's jacket is very funny and showcases his protean capacity to take on different roles in the play. Always an entrancing storyteller, at times Byron appears to be a Pied Piper figure, leading the 'rats' of the town youth astray; sometimes he seems a satirist, the scourge of officialdom and its manifold hypocrisies; at other times he is like a disheveled, poor man's Henry the Fifth rousing an army before battle or a misbegotten Lord of Misrule leading the revels; at other times, he is like a stage hypnotist. Here, the way he produces the tortoise with a flourish from his coat, makes us think of a magician performing a trick. What else, we might wonder, has this mercurial character got hidden up his sleeves.

- Programme for the Flintock Fair.

At the end of Act One Ginger brings into the clearing this programme and reads us the feast of activities the fair has to offer. Throughout the play there are regular reminders that the main spectacle – the fair – is actually happening off-stage. Rather than the play's focus being on this event, Butterworth choses instead to focus on the margins of society, on the outcasts and outsiders unwelcome by the mainstream. The references to the fair remind us that life is going on elsewhere and time is ticking by. The fair's vapid, pallid attractions and opportunistic commercialism also highlight a sense of genuine cultural loss. At one time the fair - local, colourful, authentic, rooted in the seasons - may have had meaning for the people. With floats inspired by Hollywood films such as *Men in Black II* and ersatz 'cultural' displays such as Wesley's inept Morris dancing for the six weeks old troupe, the 'Flintock Men', the fair is a shallow imitation of what it once was.

Some significant and memorable props appear at the start of Act Two, such as the Professor's wheelbarrow and its contents. Improbably, the wheelbarrow if full of garden gnomes. Lee and the Professor line up these gnomes like soldiers to defend the mobile home. Comical yes, but also reminding us again of the battle to come and the hopelessly crazed, romantic, eccentric and hopeless little group of outsiders who will face the might of the British state in the form of an army of police officers.

Costumes

Fashion changes all the time and those of you with a keen eye for trends will be able to spot what is in fashion and what's not each season. Different social groups also have associated fashions and these associations change over time. Think of the Doctor Marten boot, for instance, or pairs of Nike Air trainers. Costumes also suggest the age of characters and their social background. Think of a tweed jacket, for instance, or a pair of ripped dungarees. In Shakespeare's time the sumptuary laws were still in place. These laws dictated what people could and could not wear depending on their status in society. Fundamentally the higher your status the greater the range of clothes and material you were allowed to wear.

Naturally, some playwrights are very specific about costumes, while others are happy for directors, actors and designers to make their own choices. In some of Shakespeare's plays he does specify how particular characters should be dressed. In *King Lear*, Edgar as Mad Tom, for instance, is dressed in nothing but rags, Lear enters at one point with a crown of flowers on his head and stage directions informs us that on her return to England Lear's exiled daughter is wearing armour. Famously in *Hamlet* the prince is donned in a suit of 'inky cloak', a striking visual sign that he is out of kilter with his uncle's court.

Butterworth doesn't provide detailed descriptions of each characters' appearance or instructions for costumes. Rather he gives his principle characters a few key items of costume and leaves the rest for the actors and directors to fill in. In the prologue, we are told that Phaedra is 'dressed as a fairy'. For a moment the audience might think she is meant to be a fairy until she knowingly 'pulls a string' to make the 'wings flap'. So we are aware that Phaedra is a young girl, dressed as a magical creature, like the ones adorning the proscenium arch. Unlike dragons and trolls, fairies aren't always powerful, so we may also have a sense of Phaedra's potential vulnerability.

Strikingly different to Phaedra in her fairy costume are Fawcett and Parsons. Though of different sexes, this double act is dressed in the same way, 'reflective jacket' over a suit. They also carry a few revealing busy-body props – a case, camera and a clipboard. This is enough detail to signal that they are emblems of some sort of modern-day faceless officialdom, possibly site-inspectors or some such. The fact that they wear the same things, a uniform, neatly signals a loss of individuality. Suits signal the world of work, especially non-manual work and management level work, while reflective jackets signal health and safety consciousness, something conspicuously lacking among Johnny Byron and his unfettered and feckless friends.

Johnny Byron's dress sense is somewhat less dull and conventional. We only see his head at first, and it is crowned with a 'Second World

War helmet and googles'. Though comically idiosyncratic at this point in the play, the helmet, like the airhorn, signals that this is a man at war with society and hints at the serious conflicts to come. Photos from the original Royal Court production show Mark Rylance actually wearing a WWI helmet, and a German one at that. Perhaps the actor just thought this helmet looked a bit more striking and stylish, but perhaps it also suggests a more provocative, counter-cultural and anti-establishment quality to Johnny. The only other costume details Butterworth supplies are that Byron is 'bare-chested', indicating his animalistic qualities and disregard for social norms. According to the set designer of the Royal Court production, Rylance's costumes for Johnny were inspired by the actor's visits to West Country carnivals. Look up some photos of the production and you'll see Johnny's outfits are a striking punkishly postmodern mixture of fashions – a touch of the pirate, a little bit of romantic gypsy, the army boots of a 'crusty', a hint of native American and so on. What all these fashion references share, of course, is that they are drawn from outsiders and counter-cultural figures.

In the production it seems Rylance also takes off the helmet and replaces it with a more casual, rather rakish hat. This is not apparent from the script, but neatly fits the idea that Johnny rather takes his eye off the various threats pressing in on his woodland sanctuary. In the Royal Court production, Rylance also changed into a stylish, if somewhat dated suit, for Act Three.

The Professor we are told is 'smartly dressed', with wellies. Not only is that a rather incongruous combination, the Professor's smart dress also looks out of place within Rooster's ramshackle clearing. In his final appearance in the play, just before the closing scenes, the Professor arrives 'garlanded with flowers. Daisy chains. Flowers for buttons,' with a 'crown of blossom'. The image recalls the passage from *King Lear* when the mad old king appears wearing a crown of flowers. As for the King, for the Professor the flowers seem to provide healing. Moments later he recalls an epiphany when he heard 'Mary' and realizes, at last, that she is gone. The Professor feels unburdened, 'suddenly light', back in touch with reality – he can smell the garlic - and announces significantly that 'the winter is over'.

Ginger we are told at one point is wearing a set of decks, appropriate for his wannabe DJ status, and later he enters wearing a pith helmet, although he is unaware of the fact. Other than that Butterworth leaves him as a blank canvas for the actor and director. At various points, Lee and Davey are wearing shades, either to try to look cool or perhaps cover their rather bleary eyes. The former also appears wearing a butcher's apron, which might be Davey's as he works in a slaughterhouse, and would therefore signal their close friendship.

Memorably, when Wesley enters the clearing in the woods he is preceded by the sound of 'jingling'. This is because he is decked out in the full regalia of a Morris dancer. Though it comes from a rich, very English folk tradition going back centuries and is connected with traditional celebrations of fertility and hunting, for a modern and especially an urban audience, there is an undeniably comic element to Morris dancing. And the situation is made far more comical because Wesley isn't really a proper Morris dancer from an ancient and venerable troupe of traditional English folk dancers; no, he's the sad and lonely landlord of the local pub, gad up, at the behest of the local brewery, like a genuine Morris dancer.

But, in fact, he looks like a carnival clown. And the troupe he's dancing for, the ancient sounding 'Flintock Men', were actually only formed six weeks before the fair to help sell more beer and merchandise. Understandably, Wesley is met with universal derision. Johnny passes judgement on the commercial-driven fakery by saying, 'It's wrong Wesley. Something is deeply wrong'. However this sense of something wrong doesn't stop Johnny and his friends forcing Wesley to demonstrate his dancing skills, or lack thereof, to great comic effect later in the play.

Lighting

Lighting can be used starkly and boldly, such as in picking out a main character in a bright spotlight, or it can be used more subtly to convey mood and generate atmosphere. Intense white light makes everything look stark. Blue lights can help to create a sense of coolness, whereas yellows, oranges and reds generate a sense of warmth, even passion. Floor lights can light an actor from beneath, making them look powerful and threatening. Light coming down on them from above can cause an actor to look vulnerable and threatened, or even angelic. Changes of lighting between scenes are common ways of changing the pervasive atmosphere.

After the prologue, Butterworth gives the audience a quick, frenzied blast of a Rooster party in full swing. As the time is midnight, presumably the stage is almost dark. However, the audience need to be able to see the outline of the caravan and the wildly dancing people, so there has to be some muted light. Suddenly this scene 'blackouts' and the birdsong that follows indicates it is now morning and light. As the play is set in late April, on St. George's Day, and several characters wear sunglasses, this might suggest that the onstage lighting is bright to fit a sunny spring day. Perhaps the lighting could also reflect the slightly surreal, dreamlike atmosphere of this clearing in the woods by making the on-stage a little brighter and fuzzier than normal.

Butterworth also uses a dramatic 'blackout' at the end of Act One and again at the end of Acts Two and Three. Cumulatively these moments of sudden and complete stage darkness become ominous. As the first Act takes place in the morning and the last in the late afternoon of the same day, it would also be tempting for the lighting director to subtly make the lighting for the final scene a little darker and more sombre.

Noticeably the only time Butterworth uses non-naturalistic lighting is at the start of Act Two. In this second prologue Phaedra appears again, still dressed as a fairy, and this time is picked out, like the star of the show, by a 'spotlight' as she sings her second song. In her first prologue Phaedra 'curtsies to the boxes', thus breaking the fourth wall. Together these occasions indicate that in some senses she's escaped from the locked, interior world of the play in ways that the other characters have not, as she is aware that she is on a stage and performing to an audience. It is almost as if Phaedra exists in a different, special and liminal dimension, part of the play, but also outside it, as befits her temporarily magical role within the play of the May Queen.

Music

Music is a highly effective device for developing mood and atmosphere. In Arthur Miller's play, *A View from the Bridge*, for instance, a romantic popular song, 'Paper-Doll' is played while two young lovers dance together in front of a man who absolutely detests and opposes their relationship, and a charged, threatening atmosphere is immediately generated. In another of Miller's plays,

Death of a Salesman a flute is used as a leitmotiv for the dreaminess of the central character Willy Loman. In *Hamlet*, Ophelia's madness is signaled by her singing of subversive and bawdy songs and Shakespeare weaves music into many of his comedies.

Of course, like Shakespeare in the comedies, Butterworth sprinkles music throughout *Jerusalem*, although that verb isn't perhaps the best fit for the frequent use of 'thumping' and 'deafening' house music. In addition to the house music the following pieces of music feature at least once in the play:

- ♪ Prologue – Phaedra's singing of 'Jerusalem'
- ♪ Song 'Somebody Done Changed the Lock on my Door'
- ♪ Song 'With the merry ring, adieu the merry spring' [This is repeated four times in the play, in Acts One and Three]
- ♪ Ginger's Flintock rap [Not everyone would count that as music.]
- ♪ Davey's Song, 'Oh, where is St. George'
- ♪ Johnny sings, 'Come on, talk to me…'
- ♪ Phaedra's song, 'Werewolf'
- ♪ Phaedra 'puts on music' to dance with Johnny in the final scenes of the play.

As befits the magical May Queen, the liminal Phaedra sings a song that knowingly shares the title with Butterworth's play, a song that resonates throughout the subsequent action. Like so much else in the play the song title/ title of the play it incorporates a double perspective. On the one hand, the words of the song come from a poem by the politically radical and visionary Romantic poet William Blake [1757-1827]. The poem expresses Blake's horror at the damage he believed the industrial revolution was doing to the green and 'pleasant pastures' and to the people of England. But this poem has been taken up by the British public-school system, the very heart of the

British establishment and it is sung patriotically during the Last Night of the Proms. Hence 'Jerusalem' carries two very different, almost opposite, ideas of Englishness. Having the song sung solo by a young girl in a fairy costume adds a degree of vulnerability and fragility.

Indeed Phaedra's single, unaccompanied voice is interrupted and utterly overpowered by the sudden 'thumping music'. Tellingly, her song finishes before the word 'mills', allowing the last words - 'among those dark satanic…' - potentially to apply to the devilish racket that sends her fleeing, as if in terror, off the stage. The same 'deafening bass pumps' from the caravan as Act One begins. Once again, this music too can be interpreted in two, opposite ways. In the potentially beautiful, peaceful, pastoral setting of an English wood, this loud, electronic music is not only incongruous, it could be seen/heard as the invasion of something alien, hostile and/or unaesthetic into a natural environment, a form of extreme noise pollution, the sound equivalent, in fact, of Johnny's mobile home and all the junk collected around it. Read this way the house music exemplifies the despoiling and corrupting of a pastoral vision of England.

But on the other hand, the overly loud music could be interpreted as the sonic expression of rebellion, as the essence of intense pleasure-seeking and complete release from restraint. The music expresses a Dionysian spirit that revels in excess. The dance music could be read as an analogue for Johnny Byron himself; how we react to it is likely to be as similarly polarised as responses to the play's charismatic, larger-than-life magic-man/ lay-about wastrel and all-round troublemaker.

Johnny's choice of song to accompany the exit of Fawcett and Parsons demonstrates both his sharp wit and his apparently preternatural prescience – he just happens to have this absolutely apt song ready to play on the record player.

'With the merry ring…' is an old Norfolk song, sung each year at the Padstow Obby Oss festivities where it has two versions - a morning and a night version. The song celebrates the arrival of May and the refrain 'unite and unite' has clear sexual connotations, as befits a ceremony celebrating fertility. [Davey's St. George song is the middle section of the song.] The first time we hear the song it comes from somewhere off-stage in the 'distance'. We hear 'drums' first and then 'accordions' and then a 'hundred distant voices sing'.

'With the merry ring, adieu the merry sing
For summer is a-come unto day…

…Unite and unite
For summer is a-come unto day.'

In his stage directions Butterworth is very keen to emphasise distance, mentioning it twice within a couple of lines. This begs the question why are these voices 'distant'? Other questions soon follow, such as where are these voices coming from and why are there a 'hundred' of them and whose voices are we supposed to be hearing? And this is before we have considered why Butterworth chooses this kind of song and why this specific one with these specific lyrics. Other noises-off in the play – the tannoy announcement, the cheering of a crowd – come from the fair taking place off-stage in Flintock. So, perhaps, the simplest answer is that we are hearing the singing at the start of the fair.

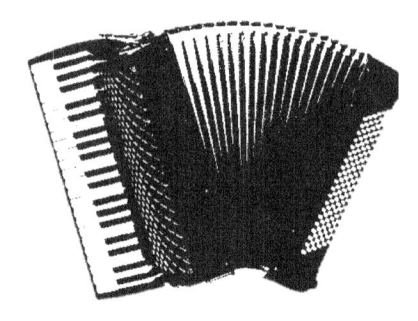

This seems to be confirmed the second time the song is sung at the end of Act One, when the stage directions state, 'from the village we hear drums and singing'. The third time the song appears is when it is sung by Davey and Lee in Act Thee after their argument about whether Lee really is going to move and leave Flintock behind. Here the song seems to be prompted by the smell in the air, perhaps the same smell that so arrests the Professor's attention a little later in the same Act and will also prompt him to singing the same song. In both cases it seems the smell is connected with nature and with something authentic, something timeless, something not touched or tarnished by the fair's crass commercialism. This acoustic folk song is connected to those ideas.

There are several qualities of the song worth considering. Firstly it's acoustic, uses traditional instruments and relies on no electronics. Secondly its repeated in the play, implying it really is significant. This repetition, like the repetition of the electronically generated house music, creates sonic cohesion, knitting parts of the play together. Thirdly the song also connects characters and, crucially, ones off stage – the distant voices – with those on stage; it is sung by Ginger, the Professor, and, in unison, by Davey and Lee. Fourthly, it is not a solo piece, it is sung by a group singing the words in unison. Fifthly, as the repetition of the imperative 'unite' indicates, the lyrics of the song itself instruct people, 'wither' they are 'going', to come and join together in happy, harmonious unity. Finally, the song is also a timeless celebration of the seasons, linking the cultural past to the cultural present, and expressing the yearly promise of summertime, a time of pleasure, play and plenty for all. In short, the song embodies a kind of authentic ideal against which the rest of which society can be measured.

As we have already mentioned, the modern-day version of the Flintock Fair appears to be a shallow, insipid and commercialised shadow of a once genuine folk custom. If, however, the singing of this authentic folk song comes from the village, this suggests that not everything about the fair has been hollowed out and commodified. It indicates that running concurrently alongside or underneath the 'Lord of the Rings' floats and the cod Morris dancing is a golden thread of something still rich and genuine, communal and celebratory.

Or perhaps the 'distance' Butterworth was keen to accentuate is both in space and time. The first time we hear them perhaps these are voices from the past. Or from another dimension outside of space and time, like the giants. Perhaps the hundred singers are like an invisible support system, even a musical army, there somewhere in the background in the clearing in the woods, waiting to be called upon.

Whatever you make of the origin of its singers, the song's expression of unity and its harmonies provide a counterpoint to the divisions in the play and the various preparations for battle that accelerate as the action develops. With the Professor's poetry, his comments on history, his evocations of Woden and Titania and story of St. George, the song weaves a tapestry of allusions to another England, an England with a deep and rich and vibrant past. This is a vision of England against which the current state of the country can be compared. And found wanting.

As it is for the goldfish whose bag is punctured by Phaedra, time is always limited. So, we will skim over Ginger's rapping, Davey's song and Johnny's singing to Phaedra's singing of the 'Werewolf'. The idea of a werewolf on the loose in Rooster's wood has already been evoked by Davey's gruesome story in Act One. Here, albeit, comically, Davey suggests that Phaedra has been followed through the woods and pounced upon. Thereupon the werewolf has 'torn her arms and legs off and eaten her virgin heart'. Ominously, as Davey is recounting this unlikely, but nevertheless disturbing tale, one of the play's potential werewolves, Johnny Byron, is splitting wood with an axe.

'Werewolf' is a plaintive type of English folk murder-ballad, written for a single voice, accompanied after the first section by a single acoustic guitar. Though the song sets out from a third-person narrative perspective, the narrator is overtly sympathetic to the poor, cursed monster and asks the audience to share this perspective, because the monstrous 'other', the werewolf, is actually 'someone, so much like you and me'. But, after the narrator hears the werewolf crying in despair that he must kill the maiden he loves, the two perspectives merge and the narrator continues in the first-person, as if he has himself been transformed: 'When I see that moon moving through the clouds in the sky/ I get a crazy feeling, and I wonder why'.

Clearly, we might associate Johnny with this simultaneously brutal and pitiful monster. We know he transforms at night into a different wilder, more dangerous and more violent version of himself, as various stories about him attest. Moreover, he cannot recall his own actions, as if they were carried out by another person or being. Think of the smashing of the TV set. In addition, Johnny is compared to a lithe, forest-loving animal, like the werewolf who doesn't 'break the branches' as he steps between the trees, and he 'bellows' like something 'feral'.

The song creates foreshadowing, lacing the comedy with a frisson of disturbing fears. Perhaps, just as the werewolf loves but kills the fair maiden, the predatory Johnny loves Phaedra, and has killed, or is going to kill her, symbolically or even literally. Phaedra singing this song also suggests that she feels sympathy for the monstrous 'other', the werewolf/Johnny, and that though she may occupy the victim role in this gothic narrative, she also knows she and the good folk of Flintock are more like the monster than they'd ever admit.

Dialogue & conversational analysis

Conversational analysis is a branch of discourse analysis used in linguistics to analyse patterns of meaning-making in human conversation. Although conversational analysis is conventionally applied to real conversations between real people in the real world, it can be easily and usefully applied to literary texts, especially to dialogue in novels and plays. Conversational analysis aims to make explicit the significance of underlying features of everyday conversational behaviour, such as variations in the length of contributions by speakers, modes of address and politeness terms, topic control and relevance, turn-taking, interruptions, asking and answering questions, and truth telling. Often conversational analysis brings to our attention sub-textual issues of power and status between interlocutors.

Think, for example, of a situation where the power and status relationships are explicit and obvious, such as a classroom. If you were to read a transcript of a lesson, how would you know that the teacher was in control, presuming the teacher was in control? Firstly, of all the potential speakers in the class, probably the teacher will speak the most and with fewest interruptions from others. Secondly, the teacher will probably speak first and last, opening and closing the discourse. We would also expect that the teacher to be in control of the topic and to set the agenda of any discussions and that she or he would ask questions that the pupils are expected to answer. In a situation where the teacher asks something like 'so how many people read Act Three for homework as asked?' and a pupil answers with something like, 'I ate all the bananas, because I really love bananas' we can readily see this isn't the appropriate response and the teacher's authority may be being challenged.

The following exemplifies how conversational analysis can be applied to any scene from *Jerusalem*.

When Troy first enters the clearing in the woods in Act Two he is like a bomb waiting to go off, brimming with hostile intent towards Johnny Byron and his band of outcasts. Taken by surprise by Troy's arrival, despite his apparently preternatural knowledge of what is going on in Flintock, Johnny seeks to diffuse this bomb. Acting like a middle-class host at a party, Johnny deploys politeness terms, such as 'good afternoon' and 'welcome', politely introduces Troy to the others and refers to him amicably as his 'mate' three times in quick succession, as well as more formally and respectfully as 'Mr. Whitworth'. The ineffectiveness of these politeness terms is indicated by how Troy responds to Johnny's friendly question, 'You win anything yet?' Rather than answering the question, as we would expect as the pattern in ordinary conversation, Troy ignores Johnny and asks his own question, 'You having a party then?' Noticeably Troy doesn't address Johnny directly with any name or term of affection.

Johnny's insistent hospitality is similarly rejected. The hyphen after Johnny's convivial line, 'let's have a drink – ', indicates that Troy interrupts and aggressively cuts him off. Whereas Johnny uses terms of affection and respect, Troy is brusquely and provocatively insulting: 'You deaf, gyppo?' Ignoring the offensiveness, once again, Johnny tries to move the conversation on to a neutral topic, asking, 'You busy today? You on the floats?' And once again, in a clear assertion of dominance, Troy ignores the question and asks his own direct and pointed one, three insistent, percussive monosyllables; 'Where is she?'

Having tried and failed with the polite approach, Johnny takes a different and more dangerous tack. His response to Troy's repeated, insistent questions seems deliberately playful and provocative: 'Phaedra. [*Beat*] Hang about. Which one's she?' That small stage direction 'beat' is important here: A 'beat' is like a hinge; it signals a slight pause in a piece of dialogue and then a move in a different direction. So far the dialogue has followed the unwritten rule of turn-taking in conversation. But, after Troy's next response Johnny switches into his familiar extravagant storytelling mode, speaking a number of lines while Troy listens. Clearly Johnny is sailing close to the wind here or, to switch the metaphor, waving a red rag to a bull. That Troy doesn't interrupt indicates perhaps that he is, momentarily at least, pushed onto the back foot. The 'pause' after Johnny's little speech is impossibly tense. And then we realise that Troy hasn't been, and won't be, deflected or diffused. He issues a short, terse command; 'Get rid of them', immediately interrupts Johnny's attempts to pacify him and resists further attempts to charm him, unrelentingly repeating the same curt command, 'Get rid of them', adding another short command, 'now' for good measure.

Finally, Troy's terseness gives way to a longer outpouring of bile. All his hatred and contempt for Johnny comes spilling out. Now it's his turn to speak uninterrupted. Whereas Johnny and his friends use expletives casually and colourfully, without meaning offense, Troy uses them as brutal weapons. The same pattern continues until the end of Act One, with first Troy and then Johnny attempting to dominate the conversation. None of the other characters present dare interrupt them. Their silence is a clear indication of their utter powerlessness in this incredibly tense, potentially explosive, situation.

The nature of the play

Like the half-and-half creatures cavorting around the proscenium arch in the prologue of *Jerusalem*, Butterworth's play is a hybrid, double form. Like Shakespeare's *The Winter's Tale* it's a tragicomedy, which, as the name indicates, is sometimes funny and other times deadly serious. However, in Shakespeare's play the tragic set up in the first half, which like Butterworth's features a lost girl, is relieved by a comic second half that culminates in the traditional comic finale - the marriage of the various well-matched couples, a symbol of restored harmony and natural order. Butterworth's play, of course, follows the reverse pattern. Entertaining, light-hearted stage shenanigans, albeit laced with a darker undercurrent, give way to final scenes of visceral, vengeful violence.

Tragedy

According to *The Complete A-Z English Literature Handbook* tragedy comes in two dominant forms:

- Greek tragedy, where fate brings about the downfall of the character(s).
- Shakespearean tragedy, where a character has free will and their fatal flaw causes the downfall.

Both definitions can be applied to Butterworth's protagonist. From early in the play it is clear that forces are amassing against Johnny Byron and that do what he may, he will not be able to escape this final confrontation. There is a sense of inevitability to how the play ends, although until its second half it's not clear that this ending will be more tragic than comic. In some ways Johnny brings this fate upon himself. If we regard him as a tragic hero, then his fatal flaw, or hamartia, could be several things – his refusal to compromise with the council perhaps being the most significant.

Does Johnny deserve to be called a tragic hero? Is his defiance of the council and the New Estate and possible protection of Phaedra heroic? Yes, in some ways. If we protest that Johnny has too many flaws to be a hero – he is after all a drug-dealer, layabout and sponger – then we could counter that all Shakespeare's tragic heroes, Lear, Macbeth, Hamlet and Othello are deeply flawed characters. In his own estimation, Johnny is a prince of the mind and he suffers a humiliating fall, like the tragic protagonists of Arthur Miller's plays, beaten up and branded on his face like an animal. However, unlike Shakespeare's tragic heroes, Johnny isn't granted a moment of sudden insight and self-realisation, nor at the end of the play does he die. Butterworth's denouement is more open-ended and ambiguous, in keeping with the nature of the play as a whole, and perhaps we don't feel the overwhelming sadness that we experience witnessing a great tragedy.

Comedy

As anyone who has seen or performed the play on stage or in class will testify, at times, Butterworth's play is extraordinarily funny. The playwright shows himself adept at creating humour through a rich variety of different types of comedy. Among others, the play features physical comedy, farce, absurdism, social satire and punchy one-liners.

The incongruous and culminative effect of the play's prolific swearing, particularly on a stage or in a classroom context, can also generate an almost hysterical atmosphere.

Physical comedy, such as the various funny dances, features prominently and regularly. Examples include: Ginger's moonwalking cum robotic dancing cum 'doing the crouch'; the whole group, including the Professor, dancing in unison at the start of Act Two; Wesley entering dressed as a Morris dancer and being forced to perform his fake fertility dance; Ginger's scene with the potentially explosive 'coconut' and Pith helmet. Sirens and klaxons going off randomly are also associated with clowning, although, as this play progresses they also develop more ominous connotations.

Farce elements include characters popping up unexpectedly, such as Lee, Pea and Tanya at the start of Act One, and Johnny's head popping out of the caravan and then moments later his appearance at the front door. At times the swift, knockabout dialogue is like a verbal form of farce. The Trivial Pursuit game and the discussion of a giant appearing or not appearing on local news are good examples.

Satire, such as the discussion of the problems with the economy prompted by Lee's attempt to buy drugs without any money to pay for them, the presentation of the council officials, Fawcett and Parsons, and the discussion of the quality of local news coverage, creates humour, but also makes a more serious point.

The Professor appearing in the clearing with a wheelbarrow full of garden 'gnomes' which are then arranged in a defensive formation is a prime example of absurdism and of the surrealist humour in the play. The discussion of whether local news would have covered a story featuring a 'ninety-foot giant' could be put into this category, as could Johnny having a tortoise on his person, stashed in his jacket. Johnny's comic anecdotes contain mundane but also absurd, ridiculous details.

Outrageous comedy, such as the full-blooded swearing, breaking of social taboos, discussion of sexual behaviour, makes us laugh almost out of embarrassment. Think of Ginger's story of how Johnny came to be barred from The Cooper's, beginning 'Then you pick up Bob Dance's pug and simulate a lewd act…'. Most of Johnny's tall stories include multiple outrageous details.

Comedy is often generated through misunderstandings. Earlier in the same scene, Johnny has tried to argue that he shouldn't be barred from the pub because he didn't start the 'fracas' involving Danny Antsey and cheating in a game of pool, only to be interrupted mid-explanation by Ginger telling him, 'That's not the fracas I'm talking about'. The professor mistaking Ginger for Maureen Pringle from the Maths department is another entertaining example.

'High comedies', such as those written by Oscar Wilde are characterised by their linguistic wittiness. Butterworth writes some great, witty one-liners that function like punchlines. For example, Johnny's suggestion that Lee's Red Indian spirit name should be 'Burns his Smurfs' or the suggestions put forward for what Wesley's Morris dance really connotes: 'I have completely lost my self-respect'; 'I need to radically re-think my values'. Another example is Dawn's deadpan response to one of Johnny's tall tales: 'You were kidnapped by traffic wardens'.

There are several running gags knitting the play's humour together. Examples include, Lee's inability to articulate his thoughts because what he's trying to say is either so funny or sad, Tanya's repeated offer of sexual favours to Lee, Johnny's anecdotes, Ginger's failure to make it as a DJ and satire based on mockery of the modern Flintock fair's commercialised vapidity. Of the latter, Ginger's description of the 'Meditation Cave' as a 'polytunnel and a massage tent' in which 'Pat Cannon is sat in there alone on a foldy chair, smoking a Lambert and Butler' is a memorable example.

There are moments in the play when the mood shifts suddenly and brilliantly from the comedic to something more serious. Lee and Davey's farewell scene, the arrival of Dawn and Marky, after Lee has started to bang the giants' drum, are examples, as, most memorably is the arrival of Troy during the quick-fire, knockabout hysteria of the Trivial Pursuits scene. More profoundly, once the audience begin to suspect that Johnny may be keeping Phaedra somewhere hidden in his caravan our laughter becomes tinged with anxiety as we wonder whether the humour of the play will become dark as midnight.

In-yer-face

'In-yer-face' is a term coined to describe theatre that presents very challenging, confrontational and shocking stage action. Usually the term is applied to overtly serious plays, such as those of Sarah Kane. Though it's a tragicomedy, *Jerusalem*'s extraordinary high expletive count and scenes of drunkenness and illegal drug-taking give it 'In-yer-face' qualities. In addition, there are the suggestions of transgressive sexual feelings – possibly incest and possibly paedophilia – as well as a final scene of horrific, brutal violence, albeit presented off-stage. Imagine watching/ reading the play with an elderly relative. That should help you appreciate its shocking 'In-yer-face' qualities.

Settings

Look beyond mere location. Setting is, indeed, the location of the action, but it is also the time era, the time of day and the socio-political setting of a play. It can also include micro-settings in terms of location – the forest and Johnny's Waterloo are two different settings. The same setting can take on more than one significance: Conceivably for Phaedra, hidden in the back room of the caravan, the woodland setting is both a sanctuary but also a prison. This double quality, so pervasive a feature of *Jerusalem*, can be very confusing reading this text, especially if you are used to the relative simplicity required for reading drama texts at GCSE level. The idea of a sort of 'Schrodinger's Vulnerable Child' – both safe and endangered at the same time is one of the glories of the play – nothing is ever quite as it seems and nothing can be taken at face value. Yet it also can be.

Location

The play is set in the village of Flintock in North Wiltshire. The village is based on the village of Pewsey, though Butterworth has changed the name, possibly to spare the blushes of some of the residents. All other place names are accurate, as are the road numbers and other elements of geographical detail.

It seems that we can take Wiltshire as a synecdoche for England as a whole. Aside from specific locations mentioned, such as Stonehenge or Avebury, which have global significance, there is little to identify the setting as having a direct bearing on behaviour or attitude, beyond its rural locale and the issues associated with poverty and a lack of opportunity for many in England's rural areas. In terms of the life faced by the teenagers in the play it could be set in Norfolk, Cornwall or

Shropshire, equally successfully. Indeed, the fact that Wiltshire sits quietly en route to many places, yet not visited by so many in its own right, makes it eminently suitable to act as an 'every-county', crossed by motorways and railways, with the lure of big cities where life really happens within touching distance, yet always just out of reach. Pewsey is on the mainline to London. It is about as far as one might commute – 90 minutes or so and the whole area, from Bedwyn to Devizes, is prized among weekenders. It is a contextual issue to be discussed how this influx alters the villages and towns. Many weekenders bring their own food and offer little to support the struggling local economy. Many seek to alter the rhythms of the villages and local papers carry articles about incomers complaining about the smell of the pig farm or the noise of the church bells on a Sunday. The old ways of rural England do seem to be changing.

The woods in Literature

Woods are profound, often mysterious, sometimes dangerous places. Even in our own times, real woods retain something of the magic and wildness they always have in stories, and most of us can recall walking in the woods at some time in our lives. It is all too easy to get lost in the labyrinthine woods, metaphorically if not literally. Woods and the forest feature in many literary texts across cultures and across time. In the *Gilgamesh* epic, for example, the monster Humbaba lives in a huge cedar forest and the most frenzied action of Euripedes' *Bacchae* takes place in the wooded mountains of Cithaeron. Time, however, prevents us from exploring within this guide the nature of 'woods' in all literature. Instead we will focus our attention on the areas which seem most relevant to Butterworth's play, specifically the woods of Ancient Greece, Norse Myth, Gothic writings and fairy tales, as well as the greenwoods of Shakespeare's plays – a primary source for much that is written and felt about this play.

Greece

In Ancient Greece the woods and the fields, the rivers and all aspects of nature were served by specific gods, goddesses and lesser immortals – naiads, dryads and so forth. What is interesting when we look at this play is the relationship evident between the woods and their self-appointed 'ruler', Rooster Byron. The woods take his name [or vice versa] and he seems to inhabit them as the Lord of the Revels – a modern Pan or other Dionysiac figure who lives his life surrounded by his followers. In this liberated space they indulge in all manner of licentious behaviour – drugs, alcohol, sex [we may presume] and other forms of wild abandon which cannot be performed in society without causing outrage and shock.

The pastoral genre, or mode of writing, emerges from the writings of Greek poets, such as Theocritus. Classical pastoral poetry features idealized peaceful idylls and fluting shepherds, not features we easily associate with the darker, more complex world of Butterworth's play. His play presents a world of illicit pleasure, of licence and of nature 'red in tooth and claw'. Yet it is also the outrageously funny and wildly energetic world of the Satyrs and Pan, dancing and singing in their revels, and, though it may be under great stress, there remains within the play some sense of the pastoral potential of the English countryside. Part of this stress, of course, comes from the supposedly civilized and modern society built on the edge of the woods. Indeed the contrast between the rural and the urban is an implicit or explicit feature of pastoral literature. In part, this modern town society appears to protect the pastoral woods from corruption by its resident troll, Johnny Byron. But, perhaps, there is a commercial motive too. Clearing the woods will help sell the newly built houses and clear a space for future potential development.

Pastoral

The Pastoral world of the Greek and Roman poets was one of peace, relaxation and escape from the urban morass of danger and immorality. When Virgil wrote his Eclogues, these were poems extolling the simple life, the life fit for a veteran of Augustus' armies who wished to settle down in peace and prosperity at the end of his military career. This writing introduces a key element of the Pastoral – that of a restorative retreat. The idea is that nature, freed from societal taint, can help to restore the soul in some way. Virgil's world is full of shepherds and former soldiers living in harmony in a new Golden Age – picking up Hesiod's descriptions of the ages of mankind from the Theogeny and the Works and Days.

Another strand which enters the depiction of the pastoral is the sense of the rural world being a sanctuary and a respite form worldly issues. This is an area which will be discussed in the Shakespeare section below, but which again seems evident. 'Johnny's onlookers' are escaping from a hypocritical, exploitative and potentially dangerous world. A world in which morality seems to be degraded. They find sanctuary in the clearing and begin to live an altogether freer, more communal and less materialistic existence. Yes, they are often intoxicated, but this seems too to hark back to a more primal time – a world in which there were clear rites of passage to progress to adulthood and a world in which society was less likely to impose strict constraints on behaviour. The short time spent in the company of Johnny by a group of teenagers can be viewed as a rite of passage, a step into adulthood. He himself stresses his role as a protector in Act One: 'They either sit in the bus stop, shivering their bollocks off, or they go to yours, or they come here'. The implication is obvious – Johnny has a role in society as part of the development of the young people – the difference is that society has placed an arbitrary ban on these rites as it has not done on the publican, Wesley, whose hypocrisy is clear for all to see: 'You get'em straight off the climbing frame and in the bloody snug'.

As it develops in art and Literature the pastoral also begins to incorporate a sense of the tainting of its supposed purity. Poussin's painting, *Et in Arcadia Ego,* shown below, depicts this notion clearly: the shepherds in Arcadia study an old tomb on which is written the Latin tag which gives the painting its name – 'Even in arcadia, am I'. The suggestion is that even in this idyllic rural location there is death, and death is lying in wait – the grit in the oyster. Inherently nostalgic, pastoral has always a sense of sadness and a sense of melancholy – it Is not all fun and games among the nymphs.

The final strands of the pastoral brings us up to date via John Clare, a poet of the 19th Century. This element is the Post Pastoral – the writing which allows the reader to explore how the farmer feels – long depicted in rural bliss, Clare would present poetry which highlighted the back-breaking nature of the work, the poverty and the hardship. We can consider the lives led by the young people in this play in this light. Whilst the early 20th Century saw a rebirth of the Pastoral as part of the Georgian movement, as writers sought to leave the potential horror of war behind them, we should also look closely at movements such as Eco-Criticism in the light of this area. This critical approach considers the effect on the planet of the actions of the farmers and the landowners and seeks to put their actions into a new context – that of the destruction of the environment. This is the crux of the debate between Fawcett and Johnny in Act Three:

Fawcett: This land belongs to Kennet and Avon Council
Johnny: Says who?
Fawcett: The law, Mr. Byron. The English Law.

Johnny's position that the common land cannot be owned and his position on it is, therefore rightful, is overturned by the rule of law – society has claimed the woods for itself and the natural has been tamed. Reading this play, we should feel a sense of moral outrage, not just about the apparent abuse of young Phaedra Cox, but also about the potential exploitation of the land itself by the council. After all, 'It's a lovely spot', says Parsons, eying its potential

Myth and fairy tale

The baby Siegfried is carried by his mother Sieglinde into the woods, to Neidhole, where the dragon, Fafnir lurks, guarding his hoard and the Ring of power. Siegfried is given over to a dwarf to be brought up who teaches him many things, but never Fear. Siegfried will be the force responsible for the catastrophe that befalls the Gods, as Wagner explores in his *Gotterdammerung* – the Twilight of the Gods.

The brothers Grimm collected stories in which innocents are repeatedly lured away from their homes and into the woods, there to face pain and sorrow at the hands of animals, family members and darker embodiments of primal childish fears - the wolf, the ogre and the witch. Other magical forest fairy tale residents include fairies, elves, trolls and dwarves, some helpful, others dangerous. Stephen Sondheim builds on Freud's exploration of the forests of the mind and explores the sorrows and hopes of the characters from those same tales. Angela Carter writes her own feminist versions of fairy tales in *The Bloody Chamber*, exploring in full technical-coloured detail the psycho-erotic nature of what lies underneath the veneer of the 'woods'. In all these texts, the woods is the dark, other place, the wild world outside the safe confines of the home, into which the child must travel to face fear, but also to conquer it and, in so doing, grow-up.

And then we read *Jerusalem*. In light of all the above, the setting of a clearing in a wood should send a few shivers down our spines. We are in the wolves' world, the dragon's lair, the witch's house and every location in the fairy tale world in which the innocent is in mortal danger. This should never be forgotten - we will each reach our own conclusion about Johnny and Troy and the issue of dragon and dragon slayer. Yes, sure, this clearing is a sanctuary – but it is also something else darker and far more frightening.

Shakespeare

We have mentioned Shakespeare regularly in this critical guide. Here we want only to look quickly at how the Woods are used in his plays – specifically, *As You Like it* and *A Midsummer Night's Dream*. Again, the idea of a setting expressing a duality, having a double nature - a sanctuary that can easily becoming a threatening prison - is clearly explored in these plays. Whilst Duke Senior flees to the Forest of Arden to escape the hostility of his brother and he gathers around him a collection of followers still loyal to his outcast cause, his eventual return to the Capital is somewhat spoiled by the melancholy Jacques who will not return. And the point is too, surely, that he has to return – the woods only offer a brief escape. Enchanting as they may be, staying longer in the woods is not a healthy option. Yes, love and free- thought flourish in the freedom the woods afford - poems are pinned to trees much in the manner described by Johnny in his response to Phaedra's question about fairies: 'I seen women burn love letters. Men dig holes in the dead of night. I seen a young girl walk down here in the cold dawn, take all her clothes off, wrap her arms round a broad beech tree and give birth to a baby boy. I seen first kisses. Last kisses...' But people are also damaged in the woods. This is especially clear in *A Midsummer Night's Dream*.

Often considered a brightly lit, jolly comic romp, this is actually a play haunted by dark shadows. Consider the woods, the fairies' playground. Fairies led by a King who seems to act out of a sense of sadistic cruelty. Into the woods rush the lovers and though they will leave the woods with their love intact, the woods are a place of separation, anguish and hatred, overseen by Oberon and his mischievous little sidekick Robin Goodfellow. Yes, we laugh and yes we applaud at the end when asked to do so, but we have witnessed cruelty and suffering which should stay with us. The woods are a setting in which much is explored about our innermost hopes and fears. No wonder they are so often a metaphor for the mind and what lies hidden in our darkest desires and fears.

Time era

The play is set in England in the present day. Written for production in 2009, this is a definite temporal location. On a large scale 2009 captures an England which was becoming increasingly aware of its own identity, post devolution and the development of Scottish and Welsh Parliaments and the rise of UKIP and the possibility of debates around an exclusively English Parliament. The BNP was increasingly powerful and there were indications that the political middle-ground status quo of the previous fifteen years was coming to an end. English Nationalism was growing in strength. The attitude explored in the 'Points West' section of the Act Two, suggests a growing feeling of irrelevance and frustration in the minds of a less educated and less 'successful' stratum of society.

Interestingly, since the play was premiered, strands of the plot have coalesced into a more meaningful pattern. Paedophilia was certainly part of the worries of society during the writing process and tabloid hounding of suspects leading to violent demonstrations was not new. The regularity of accusations aimed at celebrity figures since the play first appeared is remarkable. Starting with Jimmy Saville and moving to cover figures such as Rolf Harris, Stuart Hall and Tony Blackburn – all dating to actions alleged from the 1970s – and sportsmen such as Adam Johnson. Nobody reading this play can do so without their perception being sharpened by awareness of the atmosphere surrounding these allegations and of how often figures reviled in the press subsequently were found not to have any tangible evidence against them.

The example of Cliff Richard is useful. Despite the septuagenarian singer repeatedly stressing his innocence, he was the target of a high-profile raid on his home, a raid that featured widely in the press. Having discovered no evidence against him, eventually the case against Cliff Richard was dropped and those responsible for the orchestrated publicity surrounding the original TV coverage of the raid came under investigation themselves. A more recent case involved accusations of a pedophile ring among a group of very powerful establishment figures. After a lengthy investigation, these figures were found innocent, some of them after they had subsequently died, while the accuser was sent to jail having been proven a malicious liar and fantasist.

Jerusalem explores hypocrisy and the manipulation of society in such a way that we cannot be certain whether Johnny or Troy is the more likely abuser of young Phaedra. Once we realise that Phaedra is hidden somewhere within the clearing, we cannot be sure whether Johnny is protecting her or whether he has kidnapped her or kept her there against her will. Or whether indeed they have an illicit relationship. That said, at the end of Act Two, after her stepfather has visited the woods, Phaedra appears from the trailer, 'approaches the edge of the clearing and looks out'. She is 'shaking. Trembling. Shallow breathing'. Nothing seems to be preventing her from leaving and the most obvious source of this fear is the man who has been trying to take her back.

Set against this contemporary context is the constant harking back to antiquity in the text. Frequent mention is made of another England, an England 'before time'. Though excluded from the mainstream modern Flintock society, Johnny seems to be part of both the modern and ancient world. According to his own testimony, he chats to mythological giants 'just off the A14 outside Upavon' and here, as in many places, Butterworth links the two eras with ease through the application of utterly mundane details. At the end of the play, when Johnny calls his army to defend the site, the two worlds are about to clash. It is hard not to respond to the idea of a past 'Golden age', before society had imposed seemingly arbitrary rules and regulations and Johnny evidently belongs to such a world – he is 'heavy stone which immediately ties him to the many so-called Sarsen stones which litter the Wiltshire countryside and seem to be relics of a much older time. In the county which houses Stonehenge, The Avebury stone circle and numerous Neolithic burial barrows [another term used by Johnny, to denote a grave] the linking of the protagonist to this past era is important in establishing his right to remain outside society and to lay claim to the land.

Time when

After the prologue and the brief scene of manic midnight revelry, it is 9.00 a.m. on St. George's Day. We know this because in the opening pages we are given a clear reference by Parsons. Indeed the first word uttered in the play by these two emissaries from conventional society is 'time' as if they are bringing this alien concept into the timeless world of the woods. The sense that more than one way of measuring time is at work within the world of this play is subtly suggested by the fact we don't hear the old church bell toll nine until slightly later, implying that there is no absolutely definite 9.00 a.m., despite what Parsons' digital watch may indicate. Indeed within the woods, perhaps, there is no real, fixed or regular time. Sunrise and sunset have tended to demark the farming day throughout history. Scheduled time is a strictly urban phenomenon and seems out of place.

The stage direction at the start of the play, after Phaedra's prologue, neatly condenses time for us: 'England at Midnight...' 'music continues until... Birdsong.' And so on, until the arrival of Fawcett.

With her first word, Fawcett seems to shatter the rural atmosphere and sets ticking the countdown which will conclude at the end of Act Three as Johnny awaits the South Wiltshire. She shatters the natural pattern of things with a single word and sets a clock on '9.00 tomorrow'. Each act moves the time on. Act Two begins at two o'clock and Act Three at five o'clock, which allows for a second countdown – to the end of Phaedra's reign as May Queen at six o'clock, as the spring light fades, until the play closes at an unspecified hour with Johnny calling his army to his aid. It seems that once Phaedra and Troy have left, time loses any sense of clarity. Marky and Ginger appear briefly but there is no indication of time beyond this point. Johnny is alone in the woods and things seem to have regressed into a state of being without the intrusion of seconds, minutes and hours as he prepares for his last stand – a figure calling up the timeless forces of these isles, standing outside the constraints and restrictions of daily time.

Characters

Johnny Rooster Byron

It is said that when the great actor Richard Burbage created roles such as King Lear, nobody expected a second production of the play since none could eclipse the great man. There is something similar afoot when one considers the impact that Sir Mark Rylance has had in the role of Johnny. Butterworth has refused any film version of the play to be made publicly available and as a result, those who saw Rylance in the role in London or New York can justly say that they witnessed history, the like of which will not be seen again. Students scan see the play in an arranged screening at the Victoria and Albert Museum in London and all attempts should be made to do so because Rylance is simply extraordinary, even when seen in a little classroom on a projector screen.

Johnny is a role requiring huge stamina, great physicality and a voice capable of summoning heathen Gods or chatting about his apparent incarceration at the hands of Nigerian Traffic Wardens in Marlborough. Whether he is just an extraordinary talented liar - 'Wiltshire's Biggest Bullshitter' as Lee disrespectfully calls him - or a magical figure stemming from some form of inexplicable ancient past is something which needs to be discussed throughout any reading.

Students are sometimes resistant to the idea of a magical figure seeming to be so 'real'. Yet there's surely more to this character than we see on the surface. He drinks in superhuman quantities, smokes, takes drugs and is utterly irresponsible, reveling in his role outside society and the freedom this gives him, whether in terms of his 'rural display' with the flare gun, his 'fracas' in The Coopers' or his generosity with his paint brush and sexual favours throughout the New Esate. He

He seems to have a kind of panoptican prescience, preternaturally aware of machinations in the village and the council. He moves 'with the balance of a dancer, or animal' and, like a super-hero, 'impossibly fast'. He can read minds, anticipate questions, perform magic and channels at various times a varied cast of famous literary and cultural icons – the Pied Piper, Dionysus, Pan, Robin Hood, Falstaff, Oberon, Puck, Henry the Fifth, the Green Man, Peter Pan and more.

Johnny's mythology

Johnny is a tremendously gifted, persuasive storyteller and seems to exert great influence over others through the brilliance of his tales. These tale tales establish him as the rightful hero of his own story and weave a complex self-mythology around him:

Myth	Focus of Tale
'Girls Aloud'	Sexual Prowess sought, escape from threat. Spoken solely to Ginger, this story stands out for the self-deprecation and sense of weakness which Johnny conveys.
Resurrection after accident [1]	Told by Ginger, this is a hyperbolic story in the manner of one who bears witness to the wonders of the hero in the face of a sceptical audience.
Scallywag [from the Jake Thackeray song]	The hero shows great sexual prowess and powers, though he is not predatory, and seems to be an object of desire for a frustrated group of town housewives.
Virgin Birth	Told by Johnny himself. Butterworth works a double bluff here: No one believes the story at first and we

	know from our awareness of intertextuality that the story is not original – it derives from a 19th Century story reported during the American Civil War and reappeared in a live Tom Waits concert as the preface to his 'Train Song'. Since we know Johnny to be lying here, we need to be aware that he may well be inventing his own mythology for his own reasons. We may trust him that little bit less henceforth.
Meeting with Giants as an equal	Locks Johnny into the ancient, mythic past. Typical grounding of the far-fetched with believable mundane details. Beautifully illustrated on stage by the comparison of a cigarette lighter to Johnny himself in the stage business.
Capture and Escape	The traffic wardens in Marlborough and full of typical flourishes of Johnny as a storyteller – the animalistic use of his 'pouches' and the implausible narrow escape up the chimney mixed with the mundane detail of the snooker and the concern for the everyday life of the Traffic Warden. Dawn is entranced and her resistance overcome by this tale
The Forest	In answer to Phaedra's simple question, Johnny gives a glorious summary of his position in the forest as an onlooker and witness of natural life at its most glorious, most wretched and most supernatural.
The Resurrection (2)	Johnny's version, told to Marky, is shorn of the hyperbole and magic, but leaves the base elements intact. Johnny is preparing Marky for his role as the next in a line of Byron boys. He has no need for

Ginger's flourishes to win over the group of onlookers – this is the truth and it is remarkable enough.

Johnny & Shakespeare

Johnny can be likened to many Shakespearean characters – both Falstaff and Prince Hal, Oberon, Prospero, Henry the Fifth… Falstaff, the 'fat knight' and comic creation at the heart of the two Henry the Fourth plays is an obvious model. Johnny may not be fat and proud of it, but his drug-taking, drunkenness and general layers of abuse certainly make up for it. Falstaff – vain, boastful and surrounded by ne'er-do-wells, prostitutes and low-lifes is a man of high status, waiting to be called back to court. We do not see this aspiration in Johnny, but the storytelling, the establishment of a society of drinking **companions** **and** the ultimate rejection by society echo the fat knight. We may not actually like either Falstaff or Johnny [imagine having Johnny as your neighbour…] yet we still laugh and root for them throughout because they are consistently entertaining.

Interestingly, he can also be seen as a Prince Hal figure in terms of his relationship with Ginger. Ginger, something of a weak fantasist, looks up to Johnny throughout and craves his acknowledgement. Johnny's failure to say that 'Ginger's a DJ' is an unnecessary denial and one which Johnny uses to firmly establish himself as of a higher level than Ginger in Act One. As the play ends, Johnny assumes his Kingship and dispenses with his onlookers as he prepares for the great battle ahead.

In the preparations for battle at the opening of Act Two the echoes of Henry the Fifth are seen. A vastly outnumbered and weakened force faces an arrogant foe. Humour is gained through the description of the fortifications, with garden gnomes being lined up like some strange and comic terracotta army. Johnny addresses his troops and, though his imagery is far removed from that of Henry before Agincourt, the tone – of violence and carnage being wrought by his 'baffled beserkers' on their vastly numerical superior enemy – recalls Henry the Fifth at war. Byron lists the heroes in the manner of Henry calling the role prior to Agincourt, before Butterworth introduces the comic bathos of Ginger: 'still no one will remember who the fuck was Ginger Yates'.

Johnny is also an Oberon/Prospero figure – the ruler of the Forest and of his Island clearing. Like both he seems to have magical powers and is willing to use them. Like both, he has secrets and a potentially cruel streak. He is selfish, yet he educates those with whom he comes into contact and allows them to pass through adolescence into adulthood under his tutelage and care.

Man and myth

Looking further back, Butterworth's protagonist seems to represent Pan, surrounded by his entourage of nymphs and Satyrs under the protection of the aged Silenus – a Satyr older than the rest who seems to have lost much of his sexual powers and is often a figure of ridicule. Or he's the pagan Green Man, the embodiment of nature, fertility and the power of the natural world. This last figure is a quintessentially English figure and one who would have been at the heart of many of the pagan fertility rites which were adopted by Christians as the Spring festivals, still familiar in festivals such as the 'Obby 'Oss in Padstow, Cornwall, and which became subsumed into St. George's Day.

Davey is quite right to liken Johnny to a 'troll' and to show the displeasure of the local residents when they are faced with their new neighbour in Act One. In many ways Johnny is a reprehensible character, and we tend to laugh at him, rather than with him. Whilst the nature of some of his activities is breathtaking – our laughter is that of people who are not having to live with him on a daily basis. When faced by real purity he seems uncertain as to how to proceed. The scene between him and Phaedra in Act Three shows this well.

She emerges from the caravan and Johnny is on the back foot. His responses are fragmentary and he appears less sure of himself and more ill-at-ease around her. There is little of his bravado when faced by female authority figures such as Fawcett and eventually Dawn; rather he is the passive partner in the conversation at first. He seems genuinely at a loss for how to respond to her questions and only shows signs of the Johnny seen earlier in the play when exploring the nature of the forest in a passage of poetic beauty. As he finishes, it is she who has failed to understand his magical wonderment, puncturing the moment with a sharp reminder that time is running out: 'look at that. It's five to six.' She makes him dance with her, pulling him to his feet reluctantly and ordering him as his 'queen' to dance. There is little evident affection in the order: 'Come on Gyppo. Come on'. He dances and as he does so, Troy appears causing Phaedra to break off. For the third time in the play, Johnny has let his guard down and become absorbed by other characters. It is nearly a fatal mistake.

Further characters from fairy tale and stories suggest Johnny as a latter day Peter Pan, always destined to be deserted by his 'lost boys' and fighting against time and the powers of a cruel society, or the Pied Piper, luring children out of the village in an act of revenge against a society by whom he feels cheated.

Can we side with Johnny despite his obvious and manifold failings? Yes, we can and many of us probably do. It depends a little on our politics. He's the underdog, the counter-cultural rebel, the spirit of liberty; he's the play's chief entertainer, witty comic and grand storyteller; in some ways he's an avuncular figure to his young followers and he shows a more tender, gentle and kind side in this treatment of the damaged professor. If we are tempted to see his ultimate rejection of his loyal friend and side-kick, Ginger, as cruel and heartless, we should remember that Johnny drives Ginger away and in so doing saves him from a savage beating at the hands of Troy and his thugs and once again Johnny saves Ginger from the violent confrontation anticipated at the end of the play. And, of course, Johnny may actually be protecting Phaedra from her abusive stepfather and he takes a hell of a beating as a consequence. Though he doesn't sentimentalise Johnny, Butterworth does tip our sympathies towards him by making the representatives of mainstream, conventional society either pallidly colourless in the case of Fawcett and Parsons or viciously violent in the case of Troy.

And what of the name Butterworth choose for his charismatic, protean protagonist? Surely his first name references the lead singer of 1970's punk band 'The Sex Pistols' with whom Johnny Byron shares a charged, anarchic, aggressively rebellious spirit. Such an association links him to working class angst. His middle name 'Rooster' suggests the confident way he struts around his home, cock of the woods, the preening, dominant male. And surely his surname, Byron, evokes another rebellious spirit, the man known in his own time as 'mad, bad and dangerous to know', the aristocratic poet and taboo-breaker extraordinaire, Lord Byron. Part working class rebel, part animal, part aristocratic, lay-about, vagabond, wastrel and larger-than-life legend in his own lifetime, like the real-life person Butterworth says he based this character on, Johnny Rooster

Byron is so dangerous you can see it from space. But he is also an utterly arresting, compelling and mesmerizing figure, one who may well be a friend of the giants.

Ginger

When Ginger complains that Johnny has failed in his bond of friendship and not invited him to the 'gathering' which opens the play, he little imagines how Johnny will get his revenge – in this Falstaffian relationship, Johnny's refusal to acknowledge Ginger as a DJ marks Ginger out as the lesser role – Falstaff to Johnny's Prince Hal. He is ultimately turned away by Johnny at the end of the play, or, as we've suggested, protected from violence by him. Certainly, Ginger is cast adrift on the wreckage of the thirty years or so that he has hung around at Johnny's beck and call. The straight man to Johnny's comedian and the foil for all his jokes, Ginger has also a strong dramatic purpose since it is from him that we learn crucial details of Johnny's back story and also much of the context for the action described outside the clearing. In addition, he's a rich source of comedy himself, particularly through his interactions with Johnny, the professor and the unforgettable scene in Act Three when he returns from the fair with a potentially explosive coconut and, unbeknown to him, wearing a pith helmet.

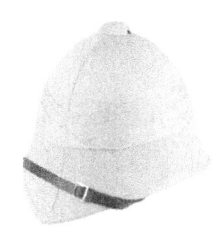

Ginger is not like the rest of the 'onlookers'. None of them show any loyalty to Johnny and it is Ginger in Act One who defends him against their scorn by telling the resurrection myth and refusing to be swayed – he was there. He saw it and will not deny his leader. At the end of the play his natural weakness causes him to run and not intervene, but for all that, his instinct is to return to help Johnny. The pain of his parting is clear for all to see. Johnny sends him away – there can be only one outcome for Ginger if he stays. Johnny's final conversation sounds like brutal reckoning, a final truth-telling: 'We're not friends. I'm not your friend. I'm Johnny Byron'. Despite Johnny telling him to 'just leave' him 'alone' Ginger is still reluctant to leave his friend, trying to argue back. Even when Johnny physically threatens him with 'the poker from the barbeque' Ginger still hesitates. Brandishing the poker again Johnny commands him to leave, 'Away I said. I ain't fooling, boy. Get away.' Finally Ginger relents, leaving with a bitter 'Once a cunt, always a cunt'.

Why does Johnny do this and say this? Surely, he's so cruel and hostile to Ginger because he's desperate to drive him away. If Johnny had been kinder to him, no doubt Ginger would have wanted to stay with him and then would have had to face the final confrontation with the police, a battle Ginger is constitutionally unfit for. Read in this way, Johnny is actually saving Ginger, allowing him to escape - an act of compassion and ultimate friendship that looks superficially like cruelty. After all, Johnny's last words to Ginger are 'get away'.

Older than the other 'rats', Ginger has been lost in the woods for many years. He has heard all these stories before and acts as a questioner allowing Johnny to retell and develop his self-mythology. Contemptuously, Troy disposes of him in one phrase – 'you lost boy?' and at the same time likens him to one of the sad children in Peter Pan. The only answer we can give to this question is 'yes'. A wannabe DJ, who cannot even secure a slot at the local pub, The Cooper's, whose landlord even rejects him as a 'standby' for the '2 Trevs', Ginger is a fantasist whose dead-end life, lacking both education and opportunity in the heart of rural England in the 21st Century is too typical of too many lost boys and girls, for whom the chance to leave has not been taken and for whom little chance of improvement is seen on the horizon. There's a lingering sadness to Ginger, despite all the laughs.

Phaedra

Phaedra opens the play, but it is not until much later that we know for sure that it is she who we have heard singing and that she is living in Johnny's van. We have no idea how long she has been there and how she got there and in Johnny – her apparent saviour – the villagers have seized upon the notion of a sexual predator putting her at risk and justifying Troy's emergence as a fire- breathing tool of societal vengeance. Yet approaching 70% of abuse is thought to be at the hands of family members and 90% at the hands of close friends, teachers or relatives. Indeed, Troy seems a far more likely aggressor in many ways and, if this is the case, Johnny is actually providing her protection.

Phaedra appears only in two prologues and the closing seconds of Act Two prior to her scene with Johnny in Act Three. In all appearances she is skittish, and either runs for shelter or is 'saved' by a blackout, suggesting a character who is frightened of the unknown and used to flight, rather than fight as a response to threat. Her solo singing – pure and innocent, especially when shattered by the rave at the opening of the play suggests an innocent time – a time of fairies, to complement her dress – and this idea resonates throughout Act One. Blake's Jerusalem is well enough known that the audience recognise the 'Dark Satanic Mills' as being represented by the Rave Music – thus establishing a threat to the peace and tranquility of a pastoral idyll, though also suggestive of the manner in which her innocence may have been shattered if the events discussed in the play are real. Phaedra establishes the sense of innocence and experience with which we watch Act One.

She also opens Act Two, ominously singing Barry Dransfield's 'Werewolf' – a folk song in which the werewolf seeks pity for horrific, murderous acts he knows to be wrong, but which he cannot help. The song echoes Davey's comic, but also gruesome discussion of Phaedra's possible fate and looks forward to the encounter with Troy later in the act. It sets up the discussion of which of Johnny or Troy may be the abuser of this innocent girl. At the end of the act she stares into the auditorium – we assume she stares into the woods – and something unseen frightens her as the blackout falls. There is no Prologue to Act Three – none is needed – Phaedra has established a coming threat as Act Two ends.

When we finally meet her in Act Three, her character seems very young. Her world and Johnny's world collide, but do no enmesh. She asks about fairies and elves and Johnny seems irritated by her childishness – instead of a brief noncommittal reply, he answers his earlier question: 'What the fuck is a English forest for?' and paints a glorious image of a forest in sorrow and in joy. Metaphorical references to Golden stags suggest a golden age, now lost to all but those lucky enough to engage with this life. If it is an invitation to Phaedra to engage, it receives no response. She is a child of the non-rural world – time is key to her, not some pastoral idyll. As she asks Johnny to dance, we may detect a childish petulance in her language and an assumption that she will get her own way – the same attitude which may have caused her to be barred from the 'Rakers as under-age or to have run away from home prior to this current period of absence. However she is viewed, as her fairy costume suggest, and in particular the fragile fairy wings, she is a tragically vulnerable figure, desperately seeking refuge in the heart of the forest. Or she has been lured like Little Red-Riding-Hood or Hansel and Gretel right into the wolf's lair or the wicked witch's house.

And what of her rather exotic-sounding, Greek name? It's certainly strikingly unusual enough to draw our attention. How many Phaedras do you know? Exactly. It can't have been a coincidence either that Butterworth chose to name her stepfather Troy, the city [located in modern day Turkey] famously besieged by the Greeks, as described in Homer's *The Iliad*. Research the various versions of Phaedra's story in classical literature and you'll discover she was the daughter of the tyrant King Minos of Crete, and married her father's Greek enemy and destroyer of the Minotaur, Theseus. Subsequently Phaedra falls in love with Hippolytus, Theseus' son by another wife and, her affections rejected, falsely accuses Hippolytus of abusing her, an accusation that results in his punishment and, in some versions of the story, his murder by his father. Clearly the ideas of illicit, transgressive love, cross-cultural conflicts, false accusations and vengeful, brutal punishment resonate with the action of Butterworth's play.

Tanya and Pea

Their names echoing Titania and Peaseblossom from *A Midsummer Night's Dream*, Tanya and Pea are a different type of young girl. We can assume that girls like this have been moving through Johnny's group since it first became a rite of passage to spend free time at this camp. Tanya is mouthy, frank and unabashed; she seems obsessed with granting sexual favours to Lee, and only to Lee, memorably saying 'if you're not going to eat my peaches, don't shake my tree'. There is no great sense of a wild promiscuity to her; perhaps this is just witty banter, a running joke between them. Or, more sympathetically, genuine affection that has to be covered by off-hand sounding sexual banter.

Of the two, as her name – a very small, common garden vegetable suggests - Pea seems to be a younger, more innocent character. And a more sensible one. This makes Troy's treatment of her all the more savage. When Pea tries to stand up for Phaedra, Troy weaponises his language to attack her. Pea shows courage here, speaking back to the obviously dangerous and violent Troy, 'Don't call me a slapper'. His response is vile and brutal; a linguistic attack that is almost physical in impact. Troy's reference to her 'cockhole', rather than the more usual 'cakehole' used later when talking to Ginger, reveals more of his character: He sees even young girls in sexually abusive terms.

Pea develops as a character in Act Two. Evidently, she has performed some form of caring act for the Professor ['there you go Professor, how's that?'] and then leads the group in the game of trivial pursuit preceding Troy's arrival. She is not wholly innocent - she takes cocaine and drinks as hard as the rest, but these are societal infractions. Her spirit is innocent and she seems to represent the typical girl from the village – the girl that Phaedra may no longer be.

Dawn and Marky

Dawn is the only character capable of controlling Johnny. She is the mother of his child and when we meet her in Act Two seems to be the only character, other than her young son, not to be enchanted by the 'Johnny' myth. She addresses him more familiarly as John, making him sound more ordinary, and she stands no nonsense, seeming to be ready for all the tricks he is likely to play. We learn nothing of their prior relationship or their living arrangements – if Johnny is not lying about having lived in the woods for years and he is supported by Fawcett's suggestion that 'this encampment has passed unchallenged since 1982', then Marky's mother must either be very young, or possibly, and more likely, one of the many villagers for whom Johnny has performed services.

As we have previously discussed, though she tries to maintain a distance from Johnny and remain an outsider - a part of conventional society with a regular job and an income - she still cannot help be attracted by him, letting him kiss her. When she looks deep into his eyes, Dawn also sees something that makes her tremble and shake uncontrollably.

As a character Dawn reveals further depths to Johnny. Despite herself, and despite the fact that they have split up, and Johnny has been an absent father to their son, she expresses genuine concern about his wellbeing and he, in return, reveals the more tender, gentle side of his character. Or the more manipulative, depending how we read it. Johnny having a wife and child also changes how the audience might view him. It is one thing for him to follow a wild, hedonistic, self-destructive lifestyle, that's his business we might think. But it is another thing when he has responsibilities in the world – a wife and a son who may suffer as a consequence.

Johnny has made much of his Byron heritage earlier in the play, including a long sequence of ever sillier claims for Byron boys, with their teeth, cloaks and knives. At the end of the play he needs to pass on the Byron blood line. His blood matters to him and Marky is the future. In Act Two, Johnny and Marky talk without communicating and all Johnny's inadequacies as a father are exposed. Pointedly, when invited to, Marky rejects the chance to give his father a hug. As a genuine innocent, a small child, in Johnny's woodland world, Marky has the power to shame his father. Like his mother, Marky also seems impervious to Johnny's charms. On the surface, Johnny may seem to be indomitable and captivating, but through Marky, Butterworth is able to show that Byron's mesmeric powers have their limits.

In Act Three, faced by the blood-soaked wreck of his father, Marky listens and absorbs his fate: The idea of care and nurture has been a sub-theme of much of the play. Immediately before this scene, Phaedra has been teasing Johnny about the need to care for the unnamed goldfish and it has been a theme of the Johnny/Dawn confrontation in Act Two. Johnny does not waste time, but tries to pass on his knowledge to his son.

Marky has got 'lost', which suggests Dawn perhaps hasn't taken great care of him. Notably, this time when invited to come to his father he does so, despite Johnny's horrific, blood-splattered state. Marky is told about Byron blood and the past. Johnny tells him the 'true' version of the resurrection myth before explaining his blood, as Romany blood, is rare and can be exchanged for money. Possibly the rather mundane explanation for Johnny's ability to exist outside society is found here: Ironically, society needs him. In an urgent paragraph ['school's a lie. Prison's a waste of time...'], kneeling before his son, as if seeking forgiveness, Johnny tries to impart some wisdom to his son before hugging him and sending him away from the coming danger to find his mother. At this point Marky simply wanders off into the woods. Johnny has checked his teeth, as one might check a horse, and we recall the passage in Act Two where Johnny refers to Byron boys lying throughout the countryside with 'their teeth sharp', ready to answer the call. Johnny seems to have judged Marky to be ready. He pours petrol throughout the caravan, either simply to destroy it, possibly aware that Marky needs a father convicted of drug crimes like he needs a hole in the head, as suggested by Dawn in Act Two, or as a possible act of self-immolation in the manner of great Viking and Mythological heroes. The quiet, introspective, bullied, emotionally damaged, but sharp-toothed Marky is Johnny's only heir.

Davey and Lee

Another comic double-act, Davey and Lee seem to sum up the lot of the male youth in rural poverty. Both are expected to be breadwinners and to conform to the societal rules established. Lee will not do so. His planned, but frustrated, emigration provides much opportunity for humour – the refrain of confusion about the day of departure, the constant offers from Tanya and the jokes about him trying to make something better of his life. Where Davey seems content to 'make paper. Shag on', Lee is utterly confused and rudderless. Lee has taken a view of life from the Internet, picking up ideas at random and is emigrating to try to make something of an otherwise seemingly dead-end life. Sadly, his life is, literally, worthless as he has been unable to sell his possessions to help to finance his journey and is facing the unknown with enough cash to last barely a week. His one-way ticket suggests the desperation – as an alternative to staying in Flintock, it is not really an option. The reality of life in Flintock is clearly presented by Davey.

Davey sums up the lot of the youth. He takes Johnny for what he can get and seems to offer little emotional involvement with him beyond what is needed to score drugs. He is accurate in his appraisal of the effect Johnny has on the village ['Free troll'] and is clearly part of a group who will use him with little compunction. Just as quickly he will film Johnny's humiliation to share around the group. He offers and expects no loyalty, unlike Lee who seems to be a figure who will be missed and who feels some sadness at his departure. In Act Three Davey declared his life to be 'unimprovable', consisting of the slaying of 'two hundred cows. Wham. What's your name and where d'you come from? [Mimes killing a cow]. Wham!'. It seems so soulless, empty and potentially cruel; the diametric opposite of what Lee seeks with his Potawatomie tribe. Yet this is all there is. It is literally unimprovable, unless one gets up and leaves the area. How aware is Davey of what he is saying? Does he really think his life is unimprovable? It seems unlikely. Hence there is an underlying sense of pathos to Davey.

In Act One the pair are contrasted further: Lee planning his departure and Davey leading the group in the denunciation of all things not centered on Wiltshire. Davey is small-minded and short-sighted with regards to life. Only Local matters. Anything else seems somehow to cheat him and trick him into what he sees as unnecessary displays of emotion. And yet, despite all this, Davey tries desperately hard to make his best friend Lee leave. Why? It seems curious, considering Davey's claims that life in Flintock is 'unimprovable'. And why doesn't Lee leave?

In their final scene, despite his acute awareness of the life-limiting opportunities available to him if he stays in Wiltshire, living, like Davey, with the 'same fucking people, going to the same shit pubs', like Davey, without even a 'pound or a saveloy' to his name, Lee confesses that he doesn't want to leave, 'I don't want to go'. Davey's response is an emphatic three monosyllables, 'Yes you do'. The dialogue pings back and forth for a few lines – 'I don't', 'you do'; 'I fucking don't', 'Tough. You're going' – before, unrelentingly Davey says he will force Lee to leave if he has to. In fact, if he has to, he will 'carry' him all the way to Australia.

It's a poignant, and despite the swearing, a touching scene, anticipating the final one between Johnny and Ginger. As such, it contributes a rough tenderness to the tonal richness of the play. Despite its impact on his own life, Davey knows his friend needs to leave Wiltshire and that Lee has the capacity to make more of himself elsewhere. In other words, Davey is acting selflessly, even nobly, sacrificing his own interest for that of his friend. Before they leave, Davey and Lee, like the Professor, stop and smell the air, as if waking to the sudden realisation that it is 'beautiful'. Perhaps, despite everything – the drug-taking, the commercialisation, the lack of job prospects and so forth - there may still the potential for something timeless, beautiful and worthwhile in Flintock, and in England.

Indeed, friendship, it seems, may be important. Davey and Lee have shown us in this little two-handed scene, that they are true, close friends. And in lives seeming to have little meaning, that is precious, something worth keeping.

Fawcett and Parsons

The two figures, another double act, represent mainstream, normative society and its power to impose its will on individual citizens. Though they are comic, busybody figures, easy to laugh at, their narrative function is more serious; they are Johnny's nemesis. Interestingly, in a play which does not give women dominant roles, alongside Troy, Fawcett has to take the role of the chief antagonist. Her name has a number of resonances – a tap for cleansing the woods, a homophonic 'force it', and the memory of a 1970's glamour actress rolled into one. The consummate official, her manner is abrupt and business-like, her way of speaking a bland, monochrome officialese. Fawcett will, we have no doubt, do her job properly. The contrast between Johnny, a wild force of nature with a technicolour turn of phrase, and Fawcett, a figure created by and for societal control, is stark.

She is shown no respect whatsoever, barked at by Johnny/Shep and eventually humiliated in Act Three by Johnny's tale of Mister [wandering] Hands at a pantomime. However innocent her explanation may or may not be, she is tainted by Johnny's chauvinistic behaviour and we may begin to feel sorry for her. That said, the triumph in her voice when she finally reads him his charge sheet – the short imperatives which allow no debate of room for a grey area – is clear to the audience and is uncomfortable. Johnny is all of these things and she has got her man. There is no room in her mind for Johnny to be anything else, or for anyone, such as Wesley, who is equally culpable, to be treated in the same way.

Her sidekick, Parsons, is the embodiment of the faceless official. A weak man, he is entirely in thrall to Fawcett and cravenly eager to please her. Perhaps he can recognise the beauty of the woods, but it may be he is just eyeing it up in terms of a development opportunity - Parsons is a jobsworth before he is a Romantic. His official job is to record accurately and document everything that takes place to ensure it is done properly. Yet, he is very willing to press the delete button when it suits him and his boss. This little act of falsification undermines his credibility and hints at possible corruption in the local council and its actions. It is his list of the names on the petition which finally breaks Johnny in Act Three.

The Professor

The Professor is the anomaly in Johnny's camp – an elderly and obviously vulnerable dementia sufferer, he provides another level of pathos and comic richness when mistaking Ginger for Maureen Pringle of the Maths department. Butterworth also uses him to recite a poem, evoke mythic and/or literary figures, such as Woden and Titania, and to deliver significant historical contexts. Hence, by providing the historical precedence, the Professor lends legitimacy to Johnny's spring revelry and to his rebellion against intrusive, busybody officialdom. The Professor's erudite contributions also help weave the rich tapestry of historical and literary allusions that give depth to the play's contemporary action, such as the repeated folk song and the story of St. George and the Dragon.

His telling of this story at the close of Act Two is a case in point. At the end of the tale, we see Phaedra emerge and run terrified into the woods, but the Professor presents an interesting question to the audience: Which the dragon and which the knight? Which the city and which the stagnant pond? Coming where it does, after the initial threats of Troy, this question must be answered. The Professor is allowing the audience a choice: Johnny as dragon or saviour and society as stagnant pond, or city threatened by the encampment. His straightforward and academic language makes this a clear choice. We decide during Act Three.

Elsewhere, his brief appearance in Act Three recalls the mad, but newly wise King Lear. He has been high and has experienced some form of pastoral epiphany, as he explains to Johnny. Acknowledging the loss of Mary for the first time, he seems to have re-established connection with the world around him, remembering the mundane detail about his gardener. Perhaps as in the Shakespeare play, the flowers have had a curative effect on the Professor. In a play full of outcasts, miscreants and leeches, the Professor is no leech. A lonely, melancholic figure, misunderstood and seemingly cast aside by society without care, he finds refuge and even a sense of community among

Johnny's rag-tag gang of miscreants. In so doing, he brings out the kind, caring and paternal side to Johnny who shields and protects him and seems to be the only character to understand intuitively what the Professor has lost.

Troy

An unflinchingly brutal character, Johnny's second nemesis, Troy appears only twice in the play. But he lurks behind much that is said or implied. His entrance is set up beautifully in Act Two as the culmination of the game of Trivial Pursuits. Whether Johnny has learned all the answers or not [the random questions make this seem unlikely] or has some kind of magical foresight, Troy's arrival in the clearing seems to remove Johnny's power. Significantly, despite his warning systems – the klaxons and sirens – his defensive lines of garden gnomes and Johnny's own preternatural awareness of what is going on in the wider world, he doesn't see Troy coming; Ginger and Lee spot him first. This little detail hints at a vulnerability that for most of the time Johnny covers beneath his Rooster bravura.

The question on which he falters is to name the poet who wrote *Jerusalem*. With the audience willing him to say William Blake, Johnny cannot remember and in doing so, it seems that he has lost something fundamental about the nature of his world. As discussed at other points in this critical guide, a power struggle ensues. Johnny seems to overreach himself, is humiliated by Troy and shown to be the victim of gross disloyalty from his followers.

Troy arrives in Act Three intent on vengeance. He has brought two companions to do his dirty work, however. Even now, society is unwilling to sully its hands with the taint of the scapegoat. Johnny is beaten and branded prior to being cast out by the very man who many will believe is really responsible for the abuse which he is blaming on Johnny. The other characters are powerless: Phaedra flees and Ginger backs away. Johnny is left alone to take on the sins of the village.

Wesley and the villagers

The sins of the village are shown in Wesley. He is Johnny's childhood friend and now runs one of the many pubs from which Johnny has been banned. As the play progresses, he becomes more than this and begins to represent the wider society and the seeming lack of comprehension of how matters could have reached this state. One of the few visitors from conventional society who come and visit Johnny in the woods, Wesley's hypocrisy is shown by his drug-taking, his exploitation by the brewery through his costume and cod dancing and his sad, depressing life by his confession to Johnny that his relationship with his wife is a sham.

Certainly, at first, Wesley is a figure of fun. His Morris dancing with all its false heritage has been foisted on him [a Swindon level decision] and he has no choice but to comply. He is a free man with absolutely no freedom. His humiliation of being made to dance for his drugs makes him a pitiable figure yet also begins to highlight the hypocrisy at the root of mainstream society. The Landlord is buying cocaine for recreational use; he is allowing under-age drinkers to drink in his pub; he grew up with Johnny and lost his virginity on the same evening in the same barn – aged twelve. Johnny will show him the apparently arbitrary nature of these rules, broken by all throughout history. Johnny's point is that the children will always break rules, drink and smoke, and at least with him, they are safe, just as their parents were before them.

Wesley is not free. He is controlled by his brewery and in Act Three we learn that he is controlled too by his wife. Sue does not appear in the play. Johnny mentions her from time to time and Wesley has a small breakdown when recalling her dominance over him: 'I went behind the bar, she told me 'hop it!" before raising the chilling idea: 'Sometimes I want to take Sue and drive her off into the middle of nowhere…' which he drops as quickly – impotent to the end. His small domestic crisis echoes that of Johnny's much larger crisis, in the same way that Gloucester's subplot echoes that of *King Lear* - both are ruined. Somehow, we feel that Johnny might be the survivor. Wesley's parting words suggest a wish to return to an earlier time, to childhood: 'I'm going up Orr Hill. Watch the trains. You wanna come?' Even his speech pattern seems to be reverting to that of childhood. Only when Fawcett and Parsons arrive does he pull himself together and revert back to his role as a steady pillar of the local community, upholding decency and enforcing its rules, telling Johnny that he's barred because Wesley runs a 'family pub' and has 'standards. Professional standards'.

As with other characters who rely on Johnny in one way or another, Wesley leans on his old friend for support when he most needs it. It is to Johnny that he drunkenly confesses his real, bitter feelings, feelings of almost existential despair. And in his characteristic rough seeming, but actually cruel-to-be-kind way, Johnny tells him what he most needs to hear: 'Go home, Wesley'. Like a mother speaking to a child, Johnny adds, 'Have a shower. Put on a clean shirt, have coffee…' Perhaps this is why, despite representing the interests of mainstream society and upbraiding Johnny for his errant behavior and expressing concern about the whereabouts of Phaedra and against his own apparent interests, Wesley has warned his old friend about the police massing to evict him. Friendships, in this play, seem to matter.

The villagers do not speak. They are reported. Their names are listed at the end of the play. It is clear that they are acting in a hypocritical manner towards Johnny, yet utterly understandable that they do so. In Johnny they see a scapegoat for their sins and they seize on the chance to drive him out. It has taken many years for them to do so and now they do not need to lift a finger because the property developers and council have joined forces to do their work for them. Pea sees no irony in the fact that she lives on the New Estate, nor does anyone else. Davey can rationalise the idea that Johnny is undesirable and that is enough for all. Only Ginger will be left utterly alone due to his age and his lack of purpose within the village – if an 'unemployed plasterer' can't find work with all the new building about to happen, then there is little hope for him.

Action

On face value, nothing much happens in *Jerusalem*. People come and go in a clearing in the wood. Mostly they seem to be just idling away their time, with little sense of direction or purpose. Granted, in Act Three an act of extreme brutality is performed, but this happens off-stage in the manner of a Greek Tragedy. Then the protagonist says his last farewells and prepares to face his final battle. We do not see the battle.

Throughout the play characters swirl around Johnny. Only at the very opening of Act Three are we uncertain where he is [he seems to be watching the action from the trees but does not intervene]. The action establishes character and purpose. Each act is a series of set pieces designed to deepen the audience's understanding of Johnny. Fawcett and Parsons are seen off by Johnny/Shep before Ginger arrives to complain about being cut from a possible party. This scene develops in the manner of an operatic ensemble as subsequent members of the cast are discovered as if by magic: 'Duet turns into trio... Trio turns into quartet... Quartet becomes quintet, and so on and on...'[1] As each is revealed so the humour broadens and Johnny can be seen developing his myths. Interaction with each character also reveals different dimensions to Johnny. The threat of impending disaster never goes away and Wesley returns to close the act with a clear warning. Against this there is the use of sound to bring the fair into the clearing: loudspeakers can be heard as can cheering, as though in ironic comment at the action on stage.

---

[1] www.script-o-rama.com/movie.../a/**amadeus**-script-transcript-wolfgang-mozart.html

In Act Two the troops are preparing for war, the defensive line of garden gnomes set-up, before all is forgotten in a game based on the 'giant's drum'. When Ginger does conjure a presence with the drum it seems to be Marky – Johnny's son, in a neat coup de theatre. The following scene with Dawn establishes Johnny's past and presents another chance for him to use his power to win over one of the followers. Marky is sent into the caravan to leave the stage clear for the two adults. He seems to spend a long time before re-emerging and Johnny does not seem to be at all worried that he might disturb Phaedra who must be in the back room. The audience do not yet know this, however, and as Dawn leaves and the trivial pursuit game begins. Troy's entrance is a shock. The scene between the two men is a masterclass in shifting power and the act ends on a disturbing note: The professor has a moment of lucid clarity and Phaedra emerges from the caravan before panicking.

Presumably she has re-entered the van before Act Three. We do not know of her presence as Davey and Lee arrive to buy drugs and/or leave a present and apologise. Repeatedly the stage directions indicate that a 'spitfire flies over', three times during the scene, reminding us both of the fair and of the imminent of battle. Before they leave, Davey and Lee are struck by the beauty of the setting. Johnny emerges from the trees. In the Royal Court production he was well dressed, ready for the denouement. In what is almost a reversal of Act One, Wesley emerges and breaks down, looking to Johnny for comfort and then Fawcett and Parsons return and deliver the final crushing blow – the petition - which is read in all its detail. The audience are constantly reminded of time passing inexorably by both the fading light and the references to time throughout the act. Left alone, Johnny is joined by Phaedra who tries to engage him in some form of affection. He refuses to dance at first before joining her in a slow dance. Her manner is provocative. She complains about the state of the room she has been in for the last few hours and has no compunction about addressing him, insultingly as 'gyppo'. It is hard to tell whether she might be flirting with him, teasing him or seeking comfort from him, for we never find out. Troy arrives and punishment is swift.

When Johnny emerges, he finds Marky and tries to pass on his message about how to take on the burden of a Byron Boy before beginning his final incantation. The play ends on an open stage direction: 'the final blow rings out and...' In some performances of the play as he is drumming, the actor playing Johnny looks out at us, as though, perhaps we are the giants who should ride to his rescue. In one version, noises-off suggest something responds to Johnny's call. There is no neat, final resolution. We are left to consider the moral and material questions raised by the play – not just about Johnny, but also about our society and the state of the nation and to wonder whether the giants will indeed come.

Style

There is much to be discussed. We are going to use three passages to discuss the style in some detail. They are the passages on pages pp. 24-30, 64-71 and 104-109 of the Royal Court script, published by Nick Hern Books. First, a note on the swearing.

The language used throughout the play is a challenge for many, especially teachers in a classroom context. This is a shame. Not only is the language an accurate reflection of the vernacular as spoken across the country, and, as such part of the play's realism, it is also the element of language which heightens and poeticises the speeches, particularly those by Johnny. It is no secret that in certain areas of the country, language is more profane than in others, also that different strata of society seem to tolerate different levels of profanity. The language used here is strong, sometimes crude, sometimes deliberately offensive. Several taboo words are regularly used to punctuate everyday speech. Perhaps the point may be to consider whether they are being used aggressively or alliteratively. It's not so much the actual words that matter, it's the tone and intention behind them. For the most part, words such as 'fuck', 'cunt' or 'twat' are not used in any way with the intention of referring to their sexual meanings. They are not used threateningly and seem to be part of everyday speech. It is only when Troy appears that things seem to change. Because we have become used to the profanities used throughout the play, Troy's highly weaponised use of the terms and his overt attempts to silence Pea and Ginger by using such language still makes us shudder.

We should be able to discuss the societal acceptance of language and try to understand why some words are taboo, yet tolerated in some areas of society. Johnny's language is richly expressive, and we should cherish the fact, whilst being aware of the sexist nature of many of the expletives. Language is as much part of the gender stereotypes in society as are any forms of dress code. This play seems to present a male-dominated society, even if Fawcett is triumphant. The girls in the woods seem to wish to be seen as no different from the boys in terms of the bad language they use. Rejecting the social pressure to be ladylike, the girls swear with as much expressive gusto as anyone else in the play.

It's important to keep an open mind on this issue of foul or bad language. As those two little adjectives imply, some people, teachers, students, readers, members of the audience will find the language of the play so offensive it will be an insuperable barrier to their appreciation of *Jerusalem*. And they have every right to feel that way, of course. But the issues need further discussion. For example, does Butterworth use this language merely for its shock value? No, for a number of reasons: Yes, it does have shock value, but the coarse language also grounds the play in its social milieu. Often it's also colourfully expressive. In addition, the play's language raises questions about the nature of societal acceptance and the imposition of arbitrary rules of 'polite' middle class society. Isn't it better to express kindness coarsely than disguise cruelty within saccharine politeness?

Analysis of extracts
1. *pages 24-30:*

This section has been chosen because of the small role played by Johnny. He is peripheral to the action, early in the play, which allows Davey and the other teenagers to explore their world and to set up ideas which will be developed throughout the play.

Davey seems to be the leader of the group in the absence of Johnny.

His language is structured rather similarly: Short sentences building through a short speech before his emotion gets the better of him: 'I leave Wiltshire, my ears pop. Seriously, I'm on my bike, pedalling along, see a sign which says, welcome to Berkshire. I turn straight round. I don't like to go East of Wootton Bassett.' So far he is in control, and like Johnny before him there is pleasure to be found in the mundane - not only is he on a bike, but he is 'pedalling along' – the small detail both conferring authenticity on the tale and allowing the audience to imagine a rather bucolic image of a familiar rustic character on his bike. But as Davey becomes more emotional, his control on his language loosens. His sentences grow in length before a rhetorical question suggests both a need for an explanation and also for affirmation from the listeners: 'Suddenly it's Reading, then London, then before you know where you are you're in France and then there's just countries popping up all over. What's that about?'

His swift shift into enquiring about Johnny's 'mates' allows a short taste of Johnny's approach to such questions. Firstly, in a typically comic self-aggrandising manner he lies ['They're MI6...'] and then he begins to develop a recurring theme - that of his longevity and his tangible link to the landscape. His sentences are short and direct and there is a brash bravado to his language: 'I ain't scared... I been running rings round that lot since before you were born. There's council officials ten years dead, wake up in cold, wet graves hollering the name of Rooster Byron...' Butterworth makes Johnny's individual speech patterns, his idiolect is very distinctive. There is the inaccurate grammar, typical of the Wiltshire dialect - the singular form of the verb with the plural 'officials', the loose, imprecise syntax – the dropping of the 'who' wake up – as well as the double adjective to add detail and realism to the graves; they're not just 'cold', but also 'wet'. We can see these souls and hear their 'hollering'. Johnny's vocabulary is wide and he is capable of choosing precise verbs for precise reasons. These dead souls do not scream or roar, theirs is a calling out, probably in anger and frustration. The image of decade-dead council officials hollering Johnny's name in their graves is a piece of incredibly vivid hyperbole, typical of Johnny, as is his giving himself such transgressive supernatural powers and his using of his own name. A typical detail too is the casual mention of his 'lawyers in New York'. It sounds entirely implausible for an unemployed layabout from Wiltshire to have such people in support. But we cannot be completely sure with Johnny.

Before the speech becomes too serious, he shifts the control and begins to question Davey about the TV. Many characters will question Johnny in this play and as we will see in Act Two, he usually manages to regain the initiative and to control the conversation. What follows now is fast and comic. Butterworth employs stichomythia, the form of rapid single line dialogue between characters, familiar from Shakespeare and before him, traceable back to Sophocles and Aeschylus. There is humour in the evident generation gap. Johnny seems genuinely mystified as the tale of the TV is played out, eventually in a phone screen. He seems unable to recognise himself and refers to himself again in the third person throughout, much as he will when telling the story of the 'virgin birth' in Act Three. Interestingly the stage directions tell us that he 'winces with every blow' of the bat suggesting perhaps that Johnny is a more sensitive character than is obvious from appearances and/or that he rather regrets his act of destruction. In any case, he is able to write off the whole event in a single line: Characteristically there is no dwelling on the incident - 'Well heard that's a complete mystery'. On the phone we have one line of dialogue, 'stand back you vermin...' which is so typical of Johnny that the audience know what he is watching. Johnny regularly refers to his 'onlookers' as 'vermin' or 'rats', helping to raise the idea of a Pied Piper figure at the centre of the group.

At this point, Butterworth increases the size of the group by the addition of Pea and Tanya. Neither are suspected of being present to this point and appear as if nothing unusual has happened. Johnny seems angry. The conversation is at surface level highly amusing, focusing as it does on the identification of the type of excrement in which Tanya has unfortunately rolled. Fox, chicken and badger excrement are discussed in stomach-turning detail: 'chicken's runnier… chicken's greener', before Johnny has the last word. Not for the last time he shows anger at the girls having stayed over: 'why don't you fuck off home like the rest of them?' Indeed he is sufficiently angry that he does not finish his lecture and grabs an axe. Ominously, as we have discussed previously in this guide, the sound of him chopping wood will permeate the following scene as the group discuss Phaedra. Butterworth will often layer action on stage with sounds from elsewhere. Here he gives three clear indications of a log splitting, almost like an aural representation of the stage direction '[beat]' which he frequently uses to enhance the effect of certain lines in the play. The axe blows fall when the absence of Phaedra for days is first established; when her age [fifteen] is established and finally when Davey presents the idea of the Flintock werewolf. The fourth and final log is split to mark the end of this section of conversation.

Johnny has an announcement and it is typical in the use of semi-archaic language, as though to give it legal status: 'Hear ye' and the continuation of the imagery of rats relating to the teenagers. The punishment is savage in the extreme. Should one of them break his rule, they will be 'strung up by the heels from the highest beech, until them's daft head pops'. Taken in two halves we see first Johnny the forest man who never mentions a tree except to name it and then Johnny the friendly figure at the centre of the group - the humour of the verb 'pops' suggesting that this might not be a serious threat after

95

all. Nevertheless, it suggests that given free reign, Johnny as a leader could become a tyrant and that his version of the 'law' might be just as self-serving as that of the council. He closes the conversation abruptly:

'Johnny Byron has spoken' as though the use of his full name carries enough weight to turn this pronouncement into law. He leaves and typically the conversation turns to discuss Johnny himself, rather than his pronouncements or any discussion of the suitability of Johnny's caravan as a place to spend the night.

The group become critical of Johnny and Davey leads the critique, though even Pea admits to being 'well embarrassed' at Johnny's drunken behaviour. There is little that can be argued with in what he says and it is the first instance of what will be revealed of regular disloyalty towards Johnny that we will see in the play. At this point Ginger, who has been peripheral to the conversation of the teenagers comes to Johnny's defence and takes the floor for the daredevil 'resurrection myth'.

2. pages 63-71

In these pages we meet Dawn, Johnny's one-time partner and the mother of his child. Her appearance is a shock. Nothing has suggested that Johnny might have family or any sense of a wider responsibility than to look after himself. This radically alters the audience's relationship with him; he is now a husband and an absentee father.

Marky's appearance, as Ginger finally strikes the drum, is a witty comment on the potential magic of the situation. It is as though a small boy has been summoned by the Giant's drum, and all are unsettled by this. Respectfully, the other characters leave Johnny alone with Marky and his mother. Dawn controls the scene at first. Her questions are pointed and direct and Johnny seems unable to respond, seeking to deflect them and to engage in banter. Possibly more importantly, she addresses him as 'John'. This use of his ordinary, 'correct' name is telling. It brings him down to earth and gives her almost a parental authority over him.

She is serious and he is under pressure. The pace is brisk with Dawn dominating the exchanges. Johnny has let her down and broken an arrangement and she attacks him, using Marky as leverage. Her stories of the abuse Marky is suffering suggest another side to the way Johnny is perceived in the wider world. He is the cause of his son's suffering. Butterworth maintains the same direct narrative style - the short sentences, often lacking a verb and this time it is Johnny who tries vainly to interrupt:

Dawn:	He can't even take his own son up the fair. Can't keep a promise to a six-year-old child.' Question: Do you have drugs in there? Where your son is.
Johnny:	Dawn-
Dawn:	Because when the police get here, tomorrow morning, what are they going to find...

The scene reminds the audience of the timescale of events – time is running out – and also places Johnny on the backfoot. Dawn's concern is more for Marky than for him. As the passage moves on, the dialogue disintegrates completely as Dawn's emotion gets the better of her. The passage clearly shows the lack of trust that Dawn has in Johnny as she deletes the number called from his phone and as she calms down , Johnny launches a subtle counter-offensive.

As he lays out some lines of cocaine, knowing how tempted she will be, he begins to tell a story – the escape from captivity myth - and Dawn is captivated. As he finishes the tale, she comes to take the drugs and the balance of power shifts completely. Dawn now speaks in single sentences and it is Johnny asking the questions. His storytelling seems to have re-asserted his control over her in a manner reminiscent of Othello and Desdemona. Now she is putty in his hands. He teases her about her knitting and finally his seduction reaches its conclusion in the three-part stage direction: 'He kisses her. They kiss. She pulls away.' The action is clear – he instigates, she accepts before ultimately rejecting his advances. She is now concerned enough to pose a huge question: 'Who's looking after you, John?' The use of his full name now seems to carry a sense of love and the wish for his protection is obvious. In reply, Jonny cites his 'onlookers' – an apt term form the 'drunk teenagers' who care so little for him in actuality. In the final sequence, Johnny asks Dawn to look into his eyes. The dialogue is spare, linked by stage directions: 'she does...she does...She is... silence' as Johnny's magic [or the cocaine] works its spell. The audience have no idea what is seen in his eyes because the scene comes to an abrupt end with Marky re-emerging form the caravan complaining about the lack of a T.V. in a neat link to Act One. Johnny produces money from somewhere and Dawn's flat 'say goodbye to your father, Marky' is suggestive of more than a simple cheerio as they leave for the fair.

As the pair leave Butterworth suggests a new side to Johnny's relationship with the woods. Stage directions tell us 'He eyes the woods nervously'. Johnny's status quo has been upset by the visit. The wood seems no longer his sanctuary and the sense that woods are places of unseen danger is raised again. Perhaps, Johnny's impregnable seeming self-confidence, is just another performance.

Marky is told to keep out of the back room. Later Phaedra will appear from the caravan. She must have been inside all the time and

Butterworth is keeping this from the audience. It is a point worth noting to discuss as part of his technique in structuring the play to keep the audience guessing and to deliver surprises throughout the action. We should also note that Johnny seems wholly unperturbed about the fact that Marky might come across her.

3. pages 98-109

In this sequence, we see several short scenes as the play reaches its conclusion. Possibly the most vital is the scene with Phaedra. Again Butterworth establishes power effectively as Johnny is changed from the aggressive and desperate man shouting into Parsons' camera, using all the archaic language we have heard throughout for moments when he wishes to establish is power – 'Salisbury white wigs', 'Hear ye' and the evocative 'there'll be blood on the chalk...' Butterworth heightens the sense of an impending battle by stressing the colour of the blood against the white chalk which is such a feature of the North Wiltshire landscape.

As Phaedra emerges, Johnny changes again, just as he had with Dawn, into a subservient role. Here he seems unsure of how best to behave. She questions him about the goldfish left by Lee at the start of the act and leads him to believe that he should be taking care of it. The stichomythia drives the pace of their discussion which slows only on page 101, when he does finally agree to look after the fish. In her questioning Johnny refers to Lee as 'A boy passed by...' implying that Lee has lost his identity as he leaves, possibly suggesting that all Johnny's onlookers become similarly anonymous once they leave him and time moves on. The conversation is humorous. But it has an echo of a missing scene – one in which Dawn and Johnny must have discussed how to care for young Marky – Johnny 'ain't got a clue' how to look after the fish, or the boy, we feel. Johnny is, however, gentle with Phaedra and saves the fish, suggesting his ultimately caring nature. Then she asks him a question which will highlight the divide between the two. In response to her query about seeing an elf, Johnny tells his most lyrical, poetic story yet.

Butterworth gives Johnny an aria, rich in simile and metaphor – a hymn to nature and to the forest which seems to answer his self-posed question, 'what the fuck is an English forest for?'. In it he talks of a rainbow setting fire to the ground, a stag with golden antlers, and seeing an 'oak tree cry'. His images reflect the life of the forest of pastoral and gothic heritage – protection and fear abound in his tale. It is a finely wrought piece of magical narration; Johnny as his most captivating. Yet Phaedra's response shows a total, lack of connection. She is not moved at all, focusing instead on 'time'. The man-made construct of time drives her to reflect bluntly: 'look at that. It's five to six'.

She tells her tale to Johnny – a tale of teenage fear prior to becoming 'queen'. Her thoughts dwell on the passage of time and her hopes of minor celebrity, now coming to an end. Expressions like 'a stomach full of squirrels' are memorable and sweet but do little to dispel the feeling that her understanding of the impact of the removal of Johnny from the forest and the subsequent deforestation is nowhere near on the same level as that of Johnny himself.

In a final moment of emotional connection she makes a reluctant Johnny dance with her: 'I command you. It's a royal command. Come on, gyppo…' Her use of the racial slur 'gyppo' throughout this scene suggests she is not under Johnny's control or, indeed, being kept against her will. They dance until she is terrified by the appearance of Troy. Butterworth uses stage directions for the action which follows.

Nothing is said, but Phaedra flees on seeing Troy. Troy issues instructions to his henchmen. In the Royal Court production Rylance turns to meet his fate, arms outstretched like a gypsy-Christ-figure ready for his crucifixion. The beating is delivered off stage, in the manner of a Greek Tragedy, before the slowly door opens and Johnny re-emerges, beaten and branded, ready to be driven off the site like a scapegoat for all the sins of Flintock. Troy bears a blow torch. It is as though the dragon has come to find St. George.

Ginger enters and tries to help before being driven away cruelly – the only time in the play when Johnny, being cruel to be kind, uses his profanities as weapons, in the manner of Troy. But there is bitter truth here too. In the swift turn of events, Ginger leaves and Marky appears – alone, apparently lost. Johnny gets the chance to educate Marky and ready him for his role as the next Byron Boy to dominate this area. He delivers his last great story – the real version of the resurrection myth. The language is calm and the images gentle: 'the ground was soft as butter', and always linked to nature. Johnny can dwell on the expectations of those who pretend to be friends: 'they want to see you shatter some bones. Swallow all your top teeth. Tongue'.

The narrative leads to the establishment of Johnny's blood as his most precious possession. On one level this is purely the Romany blood which can be sold in the hospital, but also is bloodline and heritage. He seems to be passing on this message: 'remember the blood. The blood' with the repetition and short sentences at the end of the speech exhorting Marky to remember his heritage and his bloodline, whatever may happen when his father is no longer around. As he clasps Marky Johnny's passion becomes evident. His language becomes heightened at the end of the triplet: 'school's a lie, prison's a waste of time, girls are wondrous', before dropping back into his archaisms, discussing the idea that no man has been laid in his 'barrow' wishing he'd 'loved one less woman'. The use of the archaism not only links Byron to the North Wiltshire landscape again, but also establishes a clear link with the Neolithic past, in the same manner as with the references to 'heavy stone' and the appearance of Giants.

As Marky leaves, Johnny urges him to 'find your mother'. This may be a simple instruction, but as Marky wanders off alone into the woods, perhaps, in a deeper sense, his mother is in fact nature.

Johnny is left alone and for the third time during the act a spitfire flies over the scene recalling the days when the 'few' defended England's 'green and pleasant land' from the oncoming forces of Nazism. The image possibly signals an outcome in which Johnny is victorious against all the odds, but his actions suggest otherwise. He prepares the caravan for conflagration in the manner of a great Viking sea-burial before beginning his incantation. His curse begins simply: 'May they... never sleep twice in the same bed...'- before turning much darker. His blood is used as a hideous weapon and as he turns to cursing the new-borns to be 'born mangled, with the same wounds, the same marks as their fathers'. Butterworth's language recalls King Lear as he curses the offspring of Goneril. It is heritage which is under attack and it is the heritage of the attackers which Johnny singles out for reprisal.

After this poetic passage, Johnny begins his list of names – one after another he intones the names of Byrons-dead until they merge with giants and folkloric figures of times long past. If this army ever does arrive, it will be formidable indeed.

At this point the play ends. Inconclusively. There are enough suggestions of magic to offer a hope that Johnny may well live on, as his spirit will in the figure of Marky. Doubleness and ambiguity are, however, at the heart of the whole play. With this ending, the audience is forced to continue to debate the messages and the outcomes long after the curtain falls.

Ideas

This is a play so full of 'ideas' that it is hard to know where to start. As the title indicates, it's a state-of-the-nation play, about contemporary England and about Englishness itself. The play presents Flintock, a synecdoche for England, as a bitterly divided place. On the one hand is the New Estate with its social conformities and hidden hypocrisies, on the other, the world of the woods, with its freedom and lawlessness. Which looks most like the ideal of a new Jerusalem? Perhaps neither. But of the two, Butterworth surely makes the woods seem more attractive, at least as a place of escapism. However, perhaps the pluralism is the point – both Johnny and the people of the New Estate and the local council need to be more tolerant of each other, more accepting of different points of view. A similar point can be made about the presentation of Englishness. The play presents our national identity in binary terms. Either the English are like coiled springs - buttoned-up, emotionally repressed, rule-bound, judgemental, hypocritical, uptight, living crabbed lives, or they are presented as the opposite – anarchic, hedonistic, crazy, wild.

Butterworth's use of Blake's poem also implies that such division in English society is not a modern phenomenon. And there are several different ways in which this divide can be conceptualized, such as a division between the mainstream and the non-conformist or between a puritan strain of English thought and a pleasure-seeking one. On one hand, the divide is also between commercial, corporate interests [industry, big business] and religious, spiritual, aesthetic and ecological ones. On the other hand, the divide is between the interests of society and the rights of the individual. Championing liberty, the rights of individuals and a concomitant distrust of the big state are core principles of right-wing political ideology. However, Butterworth gives the idea a powerful left-wing spin: His embodiment of freedom and resistance to the meddling state is not a wholesome, god-fearing, pillar of society nor a dynamic free marketeer. Instead, Johnny is just the kind of foul-mouthed and feckless freeloader traditionally feared and loathed by middle England, the familiar bête noire of the right-wing press.

From his own perspective, the play's protagonist, Johnny Byron, seems to be a figure locked into an existential fight to preserve the soul of England, much as Blake bemoaned its passing in the poem which gives the play its title. Where Blake saw the threat to England of the new industrial revolution, Byron identifies the threat in the rank hypocrisy of a mainstream society which will puritanically crack down on many aspects of behaviour long seen as rites of passage between teenage and adulthood, while members of this society indulged in the same behaviours themselves in the past. Through Johnny, Butterworth also gives a voice to a type of eco-criticism which considers the damage being done to nature as a result of chasing profit and the need to build homes as the population increases. As ever with the play, is, however, dangerous to try to simplify its ambiguities and resolve its double perspective into a single view. The green issue, for example, boils down to whether we view Johnny as preserving or polluting the natural, woodland environment.

The encroachment on and destruction of the green belt is widened into a Nationwide critique by the use of Wiltshire as a synecdoche for England as a whole when Davey expresses his fears of leaving his county. The attitude of 'Little Englanders' and their reluctance to accept foreign manners when abroad is a clear target. With this in mind, one can see not only a critique of NIMBYISM in this play, but also the contextual relevance of the recent BREXIT vote.

There is little doubt that Johnny is a convenient scapegoat for the village. Its members are implicated in the sinning for which Johnny is blamed. He is branded and sent from the village as though to cleanse it. The play doesn't suggest the adulterous wives and hypocritical council and publicans will be any better once he has gone, but they will have made a public declaration of their purity by this action.

The issue of paedophilia is central. There is no doubt that Phaedra is being abused, possibly sexually. However, the source of this abuse is never precisely clarified. To the village, it will be convenient to tar Johnny with this brush rather than to face the statistical likelihood that Troy – one of their own – is the abuser. Although, in one of the last scenes of the play, Phaedra's behaviour is flirtatious with Johnny and they dance together, physically close, and though the 'Werewolf' song links Johnny to the werewolf and Phaedra to its murdered maiden, Johnny's behaviour could just as easily be seen as protective and even avuncular. When, for instance, Phaedra asks him to dance, Johnny responds with 'Not on your life'. Phaedra is not to be put off so easily, though, and says, provocatively, 'I seen you looking at me'. Again, Johnny avoids the provocation and says protectively, 'You should get away, lass'. Surely, he is right. Only when Phaedra 'takes his hand' does Johnny eventually agree to dance with her. The final stage direction describing them - 'they look into each other's eyes' - is typically ambiguous. Is this disturbingly romantic, or a moment of reckoning and truth-telling? We will, of course, never know for sure.

The play's attitude to sex is mixed. Johnny and Wesley, for instance, wistfully discuss losing their virginity at twelve, clearly under-age. Johnny also boasts about his sexual conquests among the womenfolk of Flintock. Perhaps, it is merely banter, but Tanya constantly offers Lee sexual favours. The folksong repeatedly sung throughout the play celebrates sexual union. Moreover, as we've mentioned, there is a disturbing suggestion of sexual attraction between Johnny and Phaedra. Other issues involving transgression include under-age drinking and recreational drug-taking. The focus is still on the attitude of a society which places such stigma on practices which have been going on for centuries, if not millennia.

Johnny's links with a 'time before' suggest a character from a different age who sees twenty-first century England for what it is – a country defined by its materialism, by great disparities of wealth and opportunity, by hypocrisy, NIMBYISM and intolerance of those who do not conform to its values and rules. Yet we recognise that without the rules laid down by society, there cannot be safety and there cannot be security. There need to be rules in the modern world and Johnny lives outside them.

Although Fawcett struggles to gain the audience's sympathy, society needs figures such as her if it is to be safe and if it is to prosper. So perhaps, as we suggested earlier, the need is to find room in society for both ends of the spectrum. To live and live so that the Byrons of this world are tolerated, accepted and appreciated rather than treated as outcasts and shunned by all 'law-abiding' citizens.

Appendix

1. Texts

Jerusalem: William Blake

And did those feet in ancient time
Walk upon Englands mountains green:
And was the holy Lamb of God,
On Englands pleasant pastures seen!
And did the Countenance Divine,
Shine forth upon our clouded hills?
And was Jerusalem builded here,
Among these dark Satanic Mills?
Bring me my Bow of burning gold:
Bring me my arrows of desire:
Bring me my Spear: O clouds unfold!
Bring me my Chariot of fire!
I will not cease from Mental Fight,
Nor shall my sword sleep in my hand:
Till we have built Jerusalem,
In Englands green & pleasant Land.

Werewolf: Barry Dransfield

The werewolf, the werewolf
He comes stepping along
He doesn't even break the branches
Where he's been and gone
You can hear his long holler from away across the moor
That's the sound of the werewolf when he's feeling poor
He goes out in the evening when the bats are on the wing

And he's killed some young maiden before the birds do sing
For the werewolf, the werewolf
Please have sympathy
For the werewolf, he is someone
So much like you and me
Once I saw him in the moonlight
When the bats, they were flying
All alone, I saw the werewolf and
The werewolf was crying
Crying, "Nobody, nobody, nobody knows
How much I love the maiden as I tear off her clothes",
Crying, "Nobody, nobody knows of my pain
When I see it is risen, that full moon again"
When I see that moon moving through the clouds in the sky
I get a crazy feeling, and I wonder why
The werewolf, the werewolf
He comes stepping along
He doesn't even break the branches
Where he's been and gone

Scallywag: Jake Thackeray

Village scallywag, blackguard of the neighbourhood,
No good, you scandalise, your name is mud,
But it's no surprise.
They say you nick their chickens and you fish their pools,
Poor fools, if they but knew the half that you do
They'd be rather surprised.
Though your muddy boots flap, though your britches let the sunshine
inside, Susan, the parson's eldest, seems to find them irresistible.
She's only got to give you the eye, eye, eye and in the by and by

You'll be around after evensong on tippy-toe,
Tapping at her window when it gets dark.
You smoke your evil-smelling shag, and you get drunk as a newt
To boot, and this mortifies the Ladies' Institute,
Which is no surprise.
And they say you plunder their washing lines for your clothes.
God knows! If they realised what you filch besides
They'd be rather surprised.
You, your bold brown eyes, your whippy hips, your melting smile.
Winifred, the teacher at the school is not as snooty as she'd like to make out.
She knows that if she gives you the eye, eye, eye that in the by and by
You'll come early from the Pack Horse taproom on tippy-toe,
Tapping at her window when it gets dark.
You were rowdy, you were ribald at the Cricket Tea.
Dear me! By jingo! By Gad! The fella's a cad!
Well, it's no surprise.
And you've been seen to spit upon the magistrate's car!
His motor car! You'll be chastised, you go too far.
But it's no surprise.
For although Rosie, the greengrocer's girl curls her nose up as you swagger by,
Shy little slyboots, she peeps when her old man's back is turned.
She knows that if she gives you the eye, eye, eye that in the by and by,
You'll come tripping through her daddy's curly kale on tippy-toe,
Tapping at her window when it gets dark.
So don't give a toss for the gossip and the tit-for-tat
Chit-chat, they're only upset that you're not dead yet,
Which is no surprise.
And you can let them cock their snooks at you

and pooh-pooh, for, as I surmise, they envy you
And I'm not surprised.
It's no wonder when you wash your back down by the riverside
Even the local countess finds it hard to look away as you scrub.
She's only got to give you the eye, eye, eye, and in the by and by,
You'll pussyfoot through the squire's rhododendrons on tippy-toe,
Tapping at her window when it gets dark.
Ever so dark. Right dark. Scallywag.

2   Sample work

i. The following is a piece of recreative writing attempting to mimic Butterworth's and Johnny's style. Here Johnny is in his grand story-telling mode:

For fuck's sake. What? You don't believe me? Suit yourself, it's your loss you dozy cunts...

I tell you, I'm telling it straight, not a word of a lie, or I'm not a gypsy rogue and vagabond of devastatingly handsome appearance. There was me, the Byron boy himself, and her Maj. still got up in all her queenly regalia after the knighting ceremony, or whatever the fuck they call it, in some backroom of Buckingham palace sharing a packet of fags. Malb'rough lights, I recall - Big Liz having to look after those precious royal bellows, or so she claims. Absolutely gasping we were. Thirsty too. Boy can that woman hold her drink. Vodka, coke, vodka, coke, vodka, coke, little bit of charlie, couple of cans of Special Brew, a few ciders and pretty soon, her Maj has a light bulb flash of blinding inspiration. 'Byron,' she says to me, 'you're a notorious cunt as well as a liar of fearsomest renown, one what has done not a single day's honest graft in the whole of your filthy, pox-rotten existence. Would it not be a blast of the purest and choicest premium grade,' she continues in that grand regal style of hers, 'if I was to make you the most dishonourable knight that ere did wander across for this green and unpleasant land?'

To be honest, that was a little offensive - I, Rooster Byron, having once completed a full day's paid work in Devizes garden centre, and would have completed many more, perchance, but for the tragic accident with the rotary mower that sadly befell the twat of a store manager and the subsequent imbroglio with the legal fraternity - but she'd had a cider or two too many, to be frank, so I didn't like to contradict her, or stop her in the middle of the royal flow. Next thing she's only picked up a great fucking big sword. Bit wobbly on her pins, swaying from the booze and whizz, eyes lit up like fairy lights. And there's me thinking she'll either knight me or behead me, by accident or royal prerogative. Couple of moments later the immortal words issue from her royal mouth, 'Arise Sir Rooster, you filthy-minded pisshead, scurrilous layabout, purveyor of inferior quality drugs and vile corrupter of innocent children'. Now that really hurt. As God's my witness, my drugs are top quality, as you all know and can attest. Anyhow, in the shell of a nutty, that's how I came to be Lord Rooster of Byron Wood - Her Maj, in her somewhat addled state, not quite getting the title spot on.

ii.   The following essay was completed for OCR coursework.

Discuss in detail Butterworth's presentation of Johnny in this scene considering how far it is characteristic of the protagonist's presentation in the play as a whole, [pp. 67-71].

Written by Jez Butterworth and first performed in 2009, the state-of-the-nation tragicomedy 'Jerusalem' explores the jarring dissonance between deeply rooted ideas of what it is to be English versus the reality of contemporary English society. The characterisation of Butterworth's protagonist 'Johnny Rooster Byron' is an amalgamation of iconic, rebellious English figures - both real and literary - which is evident even within the character's name. This aptonym references both the counter-cultural punk-rock singer Johnny Rotten and the infamously anarchic, aristocratic poet Lord Byron. Consequently, this fusion emphasises the subversive and provocative spirit that this character embodies. However, in this scene towards the end of the play Butterworth exposes the underlying vulnerability of Johnny's character through his reaction towards responsibility and the injection of reality into his otherwise lawless and selfish lifestyle. The characteristically ridiculous story that Johnny tells to Dawn at the beginning of this scene superficially cements the entertaining charm and bravado of this character. Butterworth provides credibility to these tales through rooting the absurd plot in ordinary details. The incongruity of 'four Nigerians' all being 'traffic wardens' in the rural and caucasian town of 'Marlborough' forms the basis of this story and the implausibilities continue to pile up. An argument starts with 'shouting' and then the action escalates to Johnny being 'kidnapped' and 'tied in the basement', by traffic wardens. However, as Johnny describes the everyday occurrence of watching 'the snooker semi-finale' on the TV with his kidnappers, the addition of this mundane detail within the absurd plot of the story injects relative authenticity to his tale. Through repeating that Johnny was outnumbered by the 'four' 'big' Nigerians here, it dramatises the character's sense of macho pride as he supposedly escapes against the odds. Here, his story is used as an avoidance tactic, delaying the inevitable confrontation with Dawn. This inability to face real life and its problems strengthens the parallels between Johnny and the fictional character Peter-Pan. Through Byron's refusal to grow up, Butterworth suggests that behind the entertaining swagger and magnetism of Johnny's character is an ultimately immature and isolated figure.

Butterworth's sudden introduction of Johnny's previous partner Dawn and their son Marky at this late stage in the play is an unexpected and surprising revelation to the audience. Preceding this, apart from the emphasis upon Johnny's sexual prowess and appetite for 'Unspeakable acts' throughout the play, which in itself suggests the probability of such an occurrence, there have been no previous allusions to these important characters. Up until now, the lack of responsibility has mitigated Johnny's egotistical behaviour. However with this additional information the audience automatically reassess the situation as the actions of the anti-heroic protagonist now have tangible consequences. Butterworth explores Johnny's sense of parental responsibility through Dawn who uses Marky as moral leverage over Johnny's behaviour. The tone here is serious, as Dawn's imperative statement 'just do that for your son' pleads for Johnny to avoid being arrested by the 'South Wiltshire' police. Here, Butterworth inverts the usual grammatical function of the imperative from a demand to a plea which removes power from Dawn, indicating the intensity of Johnny's control over her. However, despite protestations from Dawn declaring 'me, I don't care' in reference to Johnny's troubling future, Butterworth makes it clear that she is genuinely concerned when she maternally questions 'Who's looking after you, John?'.

Butterworth continues to denote the complex relationship between Dawn and Johnny through the shifting dynamics of power in this scene within both the dialogue and stage directions. Dawn casually doing 'a couple of lines' symbolises her literal intoxication with Johnny and his self-governing world in the woods. Although Dawn has tried to distance herself from Johnny by building a more stable and conformist life with another man called 'Andy', in such close physical proximity to Johnny she cannot resist slipping back into old habits. The immediacy of Johnny's effect upon Dawn highlights the protagonist's magnetic and potentially corrupting nature. Initially, Butterworth portrays Dawn as the passive recipient of Johnny's attention as '*he* moves to her' and '*touches her hair*' and finally '*he* kisses her'. However, Butterworth strongly suggests Dawn's residual attraction towards Johnny and his lifestyle as her resistance of these advances is feebly given in the pathetic excuse that 'it's too hot'. Ultimately Dawn is shown to give in to her feelings as Butterworth changes the pronoun and she actively engages with Johnny and '*they* kiss'.

Arguably, despite contributing only three monosyllabic lines to this scene, Marky is the character who holds the most power here. The interaction between Johnny and his son is highly uncomfortable as Marky rejects his father's attempts to win his affection through breaking the conversational expectation of adjacency pairs. Johnny repeatedly asks rhetorical questions, the answers to which are created through embedded stage directions. The most poignant example is when Dawn and Marky are about to leave and Johnny asks Marky 'you gonna give me a hug before you go? No?'. Clearly this broken relationship is the consequence of Johnny's anarchic lifestyle and reveals that his characteristic magnetism has limits. Butterworth highlights the effect of this upon Johnny as he is ultimately left 'nervously' 'on his own'. The stage directions also reveal an underneath character to Johnny as at first 'he smiles' and then immediately 'stops smiling' connoting the pretense behind all of his previous dynamic charisma. Despite the impression of invincibility that Johnny presents throughout the play, reinstated in this scene as he patronisingly tells Dawn 'Don't you worry about me, darling', the cracks in this character's mask indicate that his outward display of bravado and charm is a performance. Perhaps through this unsuccessful interaction with his son, Johnny feels ashamed and is re-evaluating himself, as the audience has done.

The dual interpretation of Johnny's character is an underlying thematic concern throughout the play and is directly addressed in this scene. Earlier in the play, Butterworth alludes to Johnny having mythical and magical abilities through the dialogue as well as subtextually within parallels between other literary and mythological characters such as Peter Pan, Robin Hood and the Pied-piper. Here, Butterworth highlights Johnny's power over Dawn as he exerts his will, getting her to 'come and stand here' and 'look into my eyes'. This statement is repeated hypnotically, resulting in 'something' being seen deep within his eyes that makes Dawn visibly 'shake' and 'tremble'. This theatrically compelling moment on stage, where the possibility that something extraordinary occurs, actively invites interpretation but also frustrates the audience as the lack of resolution creates a sense of confusion and uncertainty. However this use of aporia ultimately provides a chance for the audience to interpret the scene independently. Although this theatrical effect seems to support a mythical reading of the protagonist, an antithetical realist reading - that he's just a charlatan - is still valid because of the ambiguity here.

Structurally, the legend of St. George and the Dragon underpins the entirety of 'Jerusalem' and foregrounds the main thematic concern of the play - the disparity between England's ancient and rich culture and the vapid state of contemporary English society. Butterworth emphasises the split versions of Englishness through extreme contrast.

Mainstream society is represented by the bland and rational council officials as well as the commercially focused New Estate, whereas Johnny and his non-conformist and rebellious Falstaffian spirit represents mysterious and mystical qualities of England's old heritage. Johnny is the underdog in this play which automatically attracts the audience to sympathise with him and his insubordination. However, the ambiguity of Johnny's motives may leave us uneasily wondering which of the symbolic roles in the legend that this protagonist represents. Ultimately, Butterworth's highly compelling atmosphere of anticipation and suspense leaves the audience questioning how Johnny will deal with the inexorable forces pressing in upon him and whether this character is the monster-slaying hero of the play or the dragon itself.

iii. The following is a piece of re-creative writing with accompanying commentary, completed for OCR English Literature NEA.

A traditional, English pub. Pieces of worn, mahogany furniture are scattered about the stage in the form of tables and stools. Behind the bar, a torn, withered English flag is draped across a mirror, the surface of the mirror riddled with crevices and cracks. Beside the bar counter is a barrel of "Wadworth 6x" ale – above that barrel, a menu of alcopops, and spirits.

Ginger sits at the counter, his figure hunched over a glass of beer. He seems tired, and like the rest of the pub, worn. Wesley is stood behind the bar, cleaning glasses and drying them with a small cloth. He puts the final glass in to a crate, and walks out of the room, crate in hand, through a door at the back of the bar. Ginger remains seated.
The door to the pub creaks open. Johnny appears.

J: Alright, Tootle?

G: Oh fuck.

Wesley walks in with a new batch of glasses to wash. He sees Johnny. He drops the crate, stunned. Glasses smash on to the floor, fragments of them cascading off into different directions. Silence.

W: Jesus Christ.

J: What? You didn't think I'd be gone for forever now, did ya'?

W: What the fuck are you doing back here?

J: Simple. I was back in the neighbourhood. Thought I'd pop round and say a quick hello.

W: It's been 2 YEARS Johnny.

J: It has indeed.

W: It's 2AM.

J: Yup.

W: Where have you been?

J: Biding my time, Wesley. Biding my time. All this hiding hasn't been for nothing. If you really knew what I'd been doing- well, you'd be surprised actually. After my brief show-down with the Council, I had to sit back. Recuperate. Get the blood flowing back through my loins.

W: Get out.

J: What? Just like that, you're throwing me to the geese? I haven't even had a pint yet...

W: I said get out!

Johnny sits down on a bar stool next to Ginger.

J: Missed this. (*Stroking the wood of the bar*) The laughing. The pints. (*pause.*) You know what really happened out there Wesley? Do ya'? I've been hearin' a lot of awful things about you Wesley, and I hope they ain't true.

W: Oh fuck off, Johnny.

J: y'see, they told me everything, after the raid. Friday it was. I was settled back, feet-up, smoking a joint, in the little armchair I have round the front of the van. Y'know – the black one? Leather? Anyhow, I'm sat there, feet up, and I start seeing these torches being shone on the hill. A bunch of 'em, like a wave of fireflies, slowly eatin' up the knoll. I start counting. 500 men, 30 dogs. All of them, coming for me. Then I hear the back-up brigade. Tanks. Panzers. Four of 'em. Saunderin' over the hill and 'ttacking from the East. They're big brutes too, mind you. Got those big rifle things on the top of thems heads. And special armour for protection. And that ain't the last of it. 'Cos ya' still have them choppers. 'Wulfs, they were. Could've called them from a mile off. Rotors cuttin' clean through the wind; proper stealth-like, soft. Could barely hear a sound. Everything was quiet, y'see? A mouse would've made more noise than them lot. (*pause.*) But what they don't know, is I can crush mice. Make 'em squeal, if I want. These hands of mine aren't coarse for nothing...

Commentary

Pride in an English heritage is a common theme within Butterworth's 'JERUSALEM'. The comma in the first line: 'A traditional, English pub' highlights this, as its function is to emphasise the word 'English' This imitates the sense of national pride that Butterworth often expresses in his play, and brings attention toward the pub's national identity.

However, this patriotism can often be undermined by society's hypocritical nature. The use of an 'English flag' concealing a mirror 'riddled with cracks' indicates that people hide the inadequate efforts made to service their past by pretending to be patriotic. The mirror's 'riddle' of crevices is particularly important, because it emphasises the EXTENT of damage that has been done to society, as the surface beneath the flag is so beaten and vandalised.

Furthermore, the perverseness of society is expressed through the positioning of 'alcopops' amongst spirits and ale. Wesley, in particular, behaves in an irresponsible way amongst the youths of society, as shown in 'JERUSALEM' as Johnny states: 'It's not like you don't serve kids.' The alcopops (which are bought by children) are being placed amongst substances that are illegal for child consumption, thus showing that society is content with breaking the law and acting cynically amongst minors.

Character themes are also emphasised in the extract, and the most obvious of these is through the comment made about Ginger. As Johnny calls Ginger: 'Tootle', there is a definite association made between the character of Ginger, and the child Tootle from the 'Lost Boys'. This promotes the idea that Ginger is lost, and struggling to find a purpose in the town of Flintock amongst the youths and adults of society – a regular dilemma for the character that Butterworth himself raises.

However, the most controversial character of the passage, and the most notorious, should not be ignored. Johnny Byron immediately creates an impression on the audience as he 'appears' at the open door of the pub. Throughout 'JERUSALEM', Butterworth portrays Byron as an ancient, and magical creature. His 'appearance', as if out of thin air, prompts further questioning of Johnny's origins, and makes the audience believe that he does possess some magical capabilities. Moreover, the mystical connotations surrounding Johnny can similarly be associated with Pan, the 'God of the Pastoral.' Although Pan is renowned for his fertility and outrageous behaviour, he still belongs to a group of esteemed (Greek) Gods that always provoked wonder and fascination, and this places further emphasis on Johnny's magical aura. Furthermore, Johnny's more rebellious attitude is emphasised as he proceeds to 'sit down on the bar stool' after Wesley orders him to: 'Get out!' This behaviour is similar to what we would see from Johnny Byron in Butterworth's original 'JERUSALEM'; instead of complying with instructions, Johnny acts in the same reckless and inattentive manner that we so often hear about, as he entertains the children with parties and drug-abusing escapades. This instance re-emphasises Johnny's constant opposition against the wishes of society, and acts as a tribute to his disobedient character.

However, one of the most important themes that is addressed through the introduction of Johnny Byron, is the case of the 'pastoral vs. Modernity'. Johnny's monologue initially utilises the same technicalities as Butterworth's 'JERUSALEM' – he speaks with continuous staccato phrases, and this sentence structure can be contrasted with his long, more elegant lines of storytelling. We can then identify the use of simile as Johnny describes 'the waves of fireflies eating up the knoll', and this emphasises the force and numbers supporting the Council. Whereas Johnny (representing the pastoral) seems isolated and alone, the Council (representing urbanity) possesses strength and men, and this links to the theme of imbalance of conflict between the technologically advanced, contemporary society, and the old-fashioned, ancient England of the past. To re-emphasise this idea of conflict, the passage also makes reference to 'Wulfs' and 'Panzers' that highlight the power of Johnny's enemies, whilst also conveniently being named after German vehicles from the Second World War. This connection with Germany confirms our impression of the Council as enemies, and even with simple technicalities such as local 'Wadsworth 6X' being positioned under the more modern alcohols of 'spirits', we can identify the most prominent theme in the passage: the fear of an overpowering, and overly destructive, urban class.

iv. The following is the first draft of a comparative essay written for the OCR specification.

Compare the ways in which Peake and Butterworth present the tension between tradition and the new in 'Titus Groan' and 'Jerusalem'.

It might seem that few texts could have less in common than Titus Groan and Jerusalem: one, a 1946 novel set in the fantastical world of Gormenghast, the other, a ground-breaking play in and about contemporary England. However, both works present tradition under threat from 'the new': the clockwork ritual of the house of Groan upset by the machinations of Steerpike; the contracting faerie-pastoral of Rooster wood and the encroaching council. One could argue that this shared theme is due to the context of the works' composition. In the wake of two world wars and a series of intellectual movements, certainties were falling like dominoes in Peake's society; around Butterworth, immigration, recession and globalisation call into question what to be 'English' means in today's world.

Jerusalem begins with Phaedra singing the eponymous hymn. As Alice Jahanpour notes, this 'immediately sets up a tension between two worlds and ideologies': Blake, whose non-conformism was repressed by contemporary authorities, and the more modern establishments which have appropriated his words to represent their own perception of Englishness. This tension between tradition and the new is fundamental to the play throughout: the vanishing pastoral England represented by Johnny, and the 'New Estate' doing the vanishing. Likewise, in Titus Groan, Steerpike climbs to the top of Gormenghast both literally and figuratively, and ancient ritual is threated with shocking consequences.

In order to analyse the tension between tradition and the new, it is first necessary to outline what the authors present as 'tradition' in their respective texts. In Jerusalem, Butterworth evokes English folk tradition and history, and in large part this is done through the use of symbols and intertextualities. As Sean McEvoy has said: 'the whole play… is suffused with traditional signs of England and its history'. Living in a forest, itself a recognised mythical location, Johnny and his friends have Shakespearean resonances: Midsummer Night's Dream ('Pea' and 'Tanya' and mischief in the woods), As You Like It; Johnny himself channeling Puck, Falstaff and Toby Belch. Specified in the stage directions, an 'Old Wessex flag' and 'Waterloo' sign reference English history passed into legend, and Johnny and his friends could be seen to evoke a Robin Hood and Merry Men-esque community. Jonny has created his own legendary ancestry, making himself out to be the last living member of the 'Byron boys', whose fantastical lineage connects him back beyond memory.

Comparably in Titus Groan: 'the estate of Gormenghast is sustained by tradition and ritual'[2]. Gormenghast operates along 'activities to be performed hour by hour... the garments to be worn and the symbolic gestures to be used' (p.66), specified to an insane degree of detail – 'at 2.37 in the afternoon Lord Groan was to have moved down the iron stairway' (p.67) – in ancient books; these rituals have not altered for time immemorial. The aberrations from tradition and wonted behaviour that occur during the novel, making up the substance of the plot, can only be recognised and understood against this backdrop of iron routine.

The two texts themselves, in their forms and styles, could be perceived as manifesting a meeting between old and new similar to that recounted in their pages. Jerusalem as a play itself 'is highly conscious of dramatic and theatrical history and tradition' (Tony Cavender), shown, for example, in the reference to 'The English Stage Company' in the scenery of the prologue, the observation of the three classical unities of drama, and the off-stage violence of the last scene in the tradition of Greek tragedy. However, it is a challenge to label the play's genre; there are comic, pastoral, and tragic elements, and abrupt tonal contrast between sections is one of the play's most effective techniques. It seems that Butterworth has cherry-picked from theatrical traditions to construct his own highly effective hybrid; perhaps in doing so, he is demonstrating the amalgam of tradition and change which is needed in contemporary England – with both Johnny and the council digging in their heels, no rapprochement is possible, precipitating conflict.

Titus Groan is similarly difficult to pin down in terms of genre – as Fred

---

[2] Anthony Burgess' Introduction to the 1968 edition of Titus Groan (Penguin Books)

Botting[3] puts it: 'the Gothic forms, like the castle and its lord... counterbalance fantasy with a grotesque glance at the nightmares of the twentieth century'. To expand upon this point: gothic tropes such as the dark castle and the insane lord rub shoulders with comic character names – such as might be found in children's books – elements of fantasy, and even bloody moments bordering on horror; for this last, one might reference the battle between Flay and Swelter, or the 'crimson wedge' (p377) ripped from Steerpike's cheek. Burgess has said that 'it would be dangerous to search too earnestly for the allegorical in Titus Groan', and in terms of reception theory, it is precisely Gormenghast's separation from the real world which accounts for its timeless relevance. However, it seems that the only way to make sense of this singular convergence of schools is by looking to historical context.

Peake, himself having fought in the second world war, experienced first-hand the violence and death scarred across Europe's consciousness. Possibly the world of Gormenghast, superficially disconnected from our own, constitutes Peake's attempt to escape the uncertainty and grief of the contemporary world into the refuge of fantasy; yet the attempt is only partially successful, as echoes of our world shadow every page. To venture one step further, there is an available interpretation of Steerpike as closely reflecting certain contemporary fears. His unstoppable rise from rags to riches, his disrespect for the establishment – terming the countess 'the old Bunch of Rags' for example – and above all his philosophy that 'equality is *everything*' (p291) could perhaps represent the threat posed by communist ideologies to Western norms. In any case, the nebulous genre of Titus Groan could be interpreted as stemming from the

---

[3] Botting, F., 1996. *Gothic*: London, Routledge.

shaken certainties of Peake's post-war period, with emerging ideologies and technologies, and above all, a recent traumatic past.

The difficulty of categorising the two texts is similar to the difficulty in deciding how the respective authors wish the reader to feel about the traditions they portray. Despite the disarming humour and raconteur-skill of Johnny, there is no doubt that he has unsavoury characteristics – poor fatherhood, drug-dealing – and that his tax-dodging lifestyle, arguably sanitised by Butterworth, is something which in reality the audience would very much like to be removed by the council. Butterworth presents Johnny in such a way that the audience can neither wholly support nor oppose him; though 'the new' of the council and estate do seem dull, Johnny's 'English folk' alternative is undeniably distasteful. Similarly, although we might condemn the apparently pointless and restrictive traditions of Gormenghast, it is clear that its residents value them, and apparently, do not wish them gone. In terms of their attitude towards tradition then, the authors are somewhat unclear.

To clarify their stances, one must turn to that which opposes and therefore defines tradition: the new. In both texts, tradition, in its various forms, is made to seem the better thing by being contrasted to a 'new' which is singularly unappealing. In Titus Groan, that which threatens tradition is Steerpike, a frankly evil character who manipulates and murders to rise to power in the castle. In this novel, what change incurs is death – Sourdust and Sepulchrave – and madness; in comparison to such a 'new', tradition seems better than it otherwise might. Similarly, to counterpoise Johnny's colourful and varied existence, we are shown the council, whose figure-filled and drab language contrasts sharply with the vivid tales told by Johnny and his friends. What tradition represents is a vibrant folk life being suffocated by the soulless uniformity of modern existence.

At this point, a discussion of the Peake's 'Dwellers' becomes apposite. The Dwellers are an 'all-but forgotten people' (p17) living in 'mean dwellings that swarmed like an epidemic' (p1) around Gormenghast, and yet they are associated with passion, art and legend – exemplified through Rantel and Braigon, the Bright Carvers, and the old man whom Keda meets, respectively. These qualities would seem to stand in direct contrast to the death-like solemnity of Gormenghast's rituals, perhaps casting the latter in a negative light. This is reminiscent of how Johnny's colourful and creative lifestyle contrasts with the dull and uniform Council, Estate, and officials. A Marxist reading might note how this relationship between primal 'life' and passion and constructed society runs along class lines in both texts. However, the Dwellers are not free from tradition either: Keda's marriage 'had been forced upon her by the iron laws', and 'immemorial custom had left Keda no option but to become the wife of… a sour and uncouth old creature' (p191). Peake demonstrates that tradition is not the preserve of a particular social group, but a fundamental characteristic of any society.

In both texts, it is arguable that tradition is already on the wane before change occurs. Sean McEvoy argues that the tradition Johnny stands for 'is already corrupted by our consumer society' and that this can be seen in the appropriation of ancient traditions for consumerist ends, like Morris-dancing as a publicity ploy for the local brewery. Likewise, 'Johnny's heroic status has already been diminished by the council's ban on dare-devilling' (Tony Cavender) and during the play we learnt that his 'friends' 'pissed' on him while he was unconscious and 'took photos with their phones' (p82) – a clear indication of his degraded status. Moreover, as a drug-dealer, Johnny participates in the consumerist society which erases communal responsibility in the interests of profit. To return to Sean McEvoy, this 'libertarian place of legend and song… has become somewhat marginal, sordid and exploitative'. In this light, the tall tales and fantasies which are so key a part of the appeal and identity of that which contrasts the council, become no more than a sad, doomed preservation of a glory that is past. However, the opposite could be argued: rather than detracting from tradition as these critics say, the evidences of waning tradition mentioned above make only more acute the threat to it, and sharpen the audience's perception of the need for it to be defended.

To compare Titus Groan, in this text there is a sense that the ancient traditions of Gormenghast are well past their zenith, quite independent of Steerpike's efforts. This is seen in the architecture of the castle, which throughout the novel is analogous to those living within it; for example, in the Stone Hall, 'the colours, once garish, have faded and peeled away and the ceiling is now a very subtle shade of grey and lichen green' (p62). The inhabitants of the castle, servants aside, interact only when necessary, and loneliness is a unifying feature of the majority of the characters – Cora and Clarice, for example, are 'suspicious of everyone and everything' at Titus' christening, as 'it had been several months since they had ventured from their apartments' (p109), and Sepulchrave only sees his wife 'when the ritual of Gormenghast dictated' (p204). The resulting lack of vitality and human affection gives the castle a dead atmosphere, and is endorsed by the advanced age of many of the characters – correspondingly, it is the 'lightness of life' in Steerpike which attracts Fuchsia, as she begins 'to hate everything that was old' (p339). Peake conveys the sense that Gormenghast is slowly dying; in this respect, the death of Sourdust is a pivotal moment, as his role of 'Master of Ritual' is taken by the unpleasant but energetic Barquentine whose accession marks an upswing in the speed of the plot.

In fact, the structure of the plot of Titus Groan is analogous to the advent of change. As the novel progresses, the speed and intensity of events increases; there is more action, and younger characters come to the fore. Change brings death, but it also revitalises the castle – for example in the replacement of the mouldering Sourdust by Barquentine. The changes which have happened are irrevocable, but the result is new life. As Sepulchrave expresses in his reverie: 'the long dead branch of the Groans has broken into the bright leaf of Titus' (p402). Titus himself represents both change and tradition – he is a new Earl, but he is of the Groan blood. Crucially, he drops the sacred symbols in the lake at his Earling – a sure sign of further irregularity to come. There is no resolution – Steerpike is alive and scheming, suspicion whispers among the characters – and neither change nor tradition 'wins', but the tussle between the two leads to a breath of life in the corridors of the castle.

In a notable point of comparison, both texts include a burning, and in both cases, it is perhaps associated with rebirth and cleansing. The library arson knocks out the pillars of tradition – Sepulchrave and Sourdust – in a symbolic destruction of tradition and history. In Jerusalem, Johnny sets fire to his caravan, his home, as part of a final incantation. Similarly, the handing down of tradition from one generation to another is a shared feature of the texts. Nicholas Phillips comments that in the last scene of Jerusalem 'a timeless ritual is enacted on stage: a father passes on his store of inherited knowledge and wisdom to his son'. The Byron boys continue, but Marky is not so complete a manifestation of them as his father, being rather on the fence between worlds. Attending school, and with his mother and her new partner firmly in the 'modern' world, Marky is a part of the society which Johnny had spurned, and yet he stands up for his father, and is the last person with whom he interacts in the play. Again, a lack of resolution. Tradition is not dead, but its future is unsure – will Marky take up the torch and be a Byron boy?

It can be seen that neither text fully resolves the tension between tradition and the new. Rather than resolving their arguments, the authors raise awareness of them. Cavender states that in Jerusalem we are shown 'a history that is in danger of being forgotten or devalued'; it could be argued that Butterworth does not show what would happen if that history is forgotten, but attempts to move the audience to the defence of it, calling into question our understanding of Englishness – as Johnny puts it 'what... do you think an English forest is for?' (p98) Nowhere in Titus Groan is the origin of Gormenghast and its tradition explained – the whole construction just *is*. As George Mann writes 'detailed scriptures and ancient regulations... give the place a real sense of oppressively looming history' – where did these scriptures and regulations come from? Possibly they appear pointless not because they necessarily are so, but because their point has been forgotten and they are carried out for tradition's sake alone. Perhaps, Peake is advocating not the removal of tradition, but continuing assessment of it.

The new is essential. Flay, once the most stalwart defender of proper ritual observance ('No change, Rottcodd. No change!' p23), exiled from the castle, goes to live in the woods where he learns to love 'the feeling that he possessed something of his own' and wonders: 'was this rebellion?' (p442). Rebellion for no purpose except one's own advancement, as we see in Steerpike, Peake clearly portrays as undesirable; by contrast, more moderate change is perhaps shown to be good – for example, the evident revitalisation of the castle as the novel progresses. As for Jerusalem, few would argue that the best way to progress is to drop everything and caravan in the woods. However, what Butterworth does elicit is a recognition of the threat that English folk tradition is under from the march of the 'nanny state'. Like Peake, he could be seen as promoting a happy medium – Johnny is the extreme, but some incorporation of what he stands for is necessary alongside the adoption of modern values.

In conclusion, it can be seen that both texts treat tradition, and develop some of the areas and issues surrounding it. In neither text is tradition perfect, but nor is 'the new' which threatens it. Rather, both texts can be seen as social critique, presenting dangers of which to be wary. Butterworth would have us take care not to lose our traditions, while Peake shows us the need to constantly reassess them.

GLOSSARY

ALIENATION EFFECT – coined by German playwright, Berthold Brecht, it reverses the conventional idea that audiences suspend their disbelief when watching a play

ANTITHESIS – the use of balanced opposites, at sentence or text level

APOSTROPHE – a figure of speech addressing a person, object or idea

ASIDE – brief words spoken for only the audience to hear

CADENCE – the rise or fall of sounds in a line

CATHARSIS – a feeling of release an audience supposedly feels the end of a tragedy

CONCEIT – an extended metaphor

DRAMATIC IRONY – when the audience knows things the on-stage characters do not

FIGURATIVE LANGUAGE – language that is not literal, but employs figures of speech, such as metaphor, simile and personification

FOURTH WALL – the term for the invisible wall between the audience and the actors on the stage

GOTHIC – a style of literature characterised by psychological horror, dark deeds and uncanny events

HAMARTIA – a tragic or fatal flaw in the protagonist of a tragedy that contributes significantly to their downfall

HEROIC COUPLETS – pairs of rhymed lines in iambic pentameter

HYPERBOLE – extreme exaggeration

IAMBIC – a metrical pattern of a weak followed by a strong stress, ti-TUM, like a heart beat

IMAGERY – the umbrella term for description in poetry. Sensory imagery refers to descriptions that appeal to sight, sound and so forth; figurative imagery refers to the use of devices such as metaphor, simile and

Personification

IN-YER-FACE – a type of play that seeks to shock the audience with extreme content

JUXTAPOSITION – two things placed together to create a strong contrast

METAPHOR – an implicit comparison in which one thing is said to be another

METRE – the regular pattern organising sound and rhythm in a poem

MONOLOGUE – extended speech by a single character

MOTIF – a repeated image or pattern of language, often carrying thematic significance

ONOMATOPOEIA – bang, crash, wallop

PENTAMETER – a poetic line consisting of five beats

PERSONIFICATION – giving human characteristics to inanimate things

PLOSIVE – a type of alliteration using 'p' and 'b' sounds

ROMANTIC – a type of poetry characterised by a love of nature, by strong emotion and heightened tone

SIMILE – an explicit comparison of two different things

SOLILOQUY – a speech by a single character alone on stage revealing their innermost thoughts

STAGECRAFT – a term for all the stage devices used by a playwright, encompassing lighting, costume, music, directions and so forth

STICHOMYTHIA – quick, choppy exchanges of dialogue between characters

SUSPENSIOIN OF DISBELIEF – the idea that the audience willing treats the events on stage as if they were real

SYMBOL – something that stands in for something else. Often a concrete representation of an idea.

SYNTAX – the word order in a sentence. doesn't Without sense English syntax make. Syntax is crucial to sense: For example, though it uses all the same words, 'the man eats the fish' is not the same as 'the fish eats the man'

TRAGEDY – a play that ends with the deaths of the main characters

UNITIES – A description of tragic structure by Aristotle that relates to three elements of time, place and action

WELL-MADE PLAY – a type of play that follows specific conventions so that its action looks and feels realistic.

About the authors

Former Head of English and now an Assistant Head Teacher, Jonathan Peel, has an Honours Degree in Classics from King's College, London and a Postgraduate Diploma in Opera Studies from the RSAMD [now RCS] in Glasgow. Prior to becoming a teacher, Jonathan worked as a freelance Opera Singer, singing roles throughout Europe and in the USA. He is an edu-blogger at the website: www.jwpblog.com where he posts resources and articles on a wide range of texts.

Head of English and freelance writer, Neil Bowen has a Masters Degree in Literature & Education from Cambridge University and is a member of Ofqual's experts panel for English. He is the author of *The Art of Writing English Essays for GCSE*, co-author of *The Art of Writing English Essays for A-level and Beyond*, *The Art of Poetry* & *The Art of Drama* series. Neil runs the peripeteia project, bridging the gap between A-level and degree level English courses www.peripeteia.webs.com, and delivers talks at GCSE & A-level student conferences for The Training Partnership.

With special thanks to our students, Rosa, Tom and Susanna, for granting permission to use their work.

Printed in Great Britain
by Amazon